NEST

The Art of Birds

NEST

The Art of Birds

JANINE BURKE

ALLEN&UNWIN

First published in Australia in 2012 by Allen & Unwin

This paperback edition published in Great Britain in 2014 by Allen & Unwin

Allen & Unwin
c/o Atlantic Books
Ormond House
26–27 Boswell Street
London WC1N 3JZ
Phone: 020 7269 1610
Fax: 020 7430 0916
Email: UK@allenandunwin.com
Web: www.allenandunwin.co.uk

A CIP catalogue record for this book is available from the British Library.

ISBN 978 1 76011 089 5

Internal design by Lisa White
Cover image and internal illustrations from *Orchard Oriole* (Plate XLII), by John James Audubon, 1831
Index by Puddingburn
Set in 12/18 pt Minion Pro by Bookhouse, Sydney

Printed in Great Britain by TJ International Ltd, Padstow, Cornwall

10 9 8 7 6 5 4 3 2 1

To Suzanne Heywood,
who also knew Sister Anthony

Contents

1
At the museum

I'm a very amateur naturalist. I trained as an art historian, not a scientist, and what I've learned about birds is from observation—often of the most ordinary suburban kind, or on holidays in the country—or from reading, or watching nature programs on TV. I bought my first pair of binoculars not long ago. As my interest has grown, my eyes have become keener. On travels in Europe, America, Australia and Africa, I have watched birds with increasing fascination and admiration. Or noted with alarm their depleted numbers. There are no sparrows left in central London, for example, because the bugs the sparrows feed their babies have gone, so the sparrows had to leave too. Pigeons can endure modern metropolitan life and you will find them trundling beside you on the street, our slightly bedraggled fellow citizens. Pigeons enraged Italian writer Italo Calvino, who declared them 'a degenerate progeny, filthy and infected, neither domestic nor wild' and bewailed that the sky of Rome had fallen under their dominion.[1] But we should not be too disdainful of this species. Their skills as messengers contributed to the French victory against the Germans at the 1914 Battle of the Marne, and during the Second World War the British Army's Air Ministry included a pigeon section. Some of its flock were awarded medals for bravery.

We tend to take birds for granted, in the landscape or in our neighbourhoods. Yet when they're gone, it's as though there's a hole in the sky, in the air, an absence of beauty and grace, and vivid chatter or haunting cries are replaced with eerie silence. The presence of birds communicates the health of a place. They are our contact with wild nature.

The lives of birds have little to do with us directly. They recognise us as predators. Apart from that, they don't need to see us. They don't need us; we don't have anything to teach them—though we can be helpful. I live with birds quite literally: a family of Indian mynas has nested in the air vent in the wall of my study. An excellent position on the second floor, it offers unobstructed views of the surrounding terrain, sea breezes as well as shelter. *Location, location, location* could be the birds' motto.

Common mynas, introduced to Australia from southern India in the 1860s, are generally disliked due to their aggressive behaviour. The yellow patch of bare skin surrounding their glaring eyes resembles a bandit's mask. I once saw a group of them dive-bomb Prospero, my cat, on the front stairs of my apartment block. I'm not sure whether it was retribution for crimes committed or whether they were merely warning him, but he did not use the front stairs again for some time. Often when I'm in the yard, hanging out the washing or getting in the car, the mynas gather on the roof to shriek at me. I yell back, 'I'm your landlady! How dare you! I'll throw you out!' In fact, we have been happily cohabiting for several years. Proximity has softened my attitude. Their bad temper is only for outside, for real and perceived threats. At home, in their nest, their tones are dulcet as they quietly confer at morning and evening. Like the mynas, many bird species have adopted our structures as their own. Mynas mate for life and my neighbours seem a contented couple. They must hear me, clattering away on the keyboard, answering the phone, reading sentences aloud, cursing when the words don't flow, but I present no danger. We listen to one another's languages without understanding but also without demur.

Where did swallows live before there were buildings? The easiest way to locate one of their elegant mud homes is to examine the eaves of your house or any other vertical construction, and there you might find, fixed to the wall and protected by an overhanging beam, a neat triangular cupped shape. You might also spot some bright eyes peering back at you or the shaft of a blue-black feathered tail. Swallows rebuild their nests, the same couple often returning to refurbish and breed after their annual migration. The site of the nest can appear perilously exposed. There's a swallow's nest attached to a wall near a cafeteria at Melbourne's Monash University, where I work. By day it's a noisy, subterranean, fluorescent-lit corridor, one of the university's pedestrian arteries. The nest, about two metres from the ground, looks vulnerable; the broom of a zealous cleaner or a missile tossed by a prankster could damage or dislodge it. I approach the nest with trepidation and each time feel relieved to see it intact. It's easy to feel protective towards nests: they are such flamboyant little miracles of design.

I can't spot the swallows' nests in Elsternwick Park, close to where I live, because they're too well hidden. But I know approximately where they are because the swallows begin to circle me with dizzying speed, a tactic meant to deflect intruders. Swallows are inoffensive birds, but to have dozens of them wheeling around your feet and face can be an unnerving experience.

Elwood, lush, low lying and close to the sea, was once a swamp and, like most of the suburb, Elsternwick Park is reclaimed land. It's a great green swathe ringed by river red gums and it has a children's playground, sports ovals and a manmade lake occupied by ducks and a family of black swans. (The lake was dug to manage the floods that periodically deluge Elwood. In the nineteenth century, before the bridges were built, folk often drowned at night trying to get from Elwood to St Kilda. They'd set off for the lights of Barkly Street and that was the last anyone ever saw of them.) Though the park seems dominated by team sports and people with dogs, the swans provide the true centre. They are worshipped like gods by the locals, who gaze in awe as the family glides in magnificent tandem from their reed-enclosed nest on the lake's island. Two winters ago when the female was savaged by a dog who'd scaled the fence which surrounds the lake, the communal outcry was hurt and real. The dog and his hapless owner were threatened with banishment and retribution. In fact, the swan initially survived her wounds. It was a shock, the awful indelible memory of what had happened to her that left her lingering for weeks and finally killed her. Swans mate for life and the male has remained with their brood, the haughty widower of the lake.

By contrast, when the turtle doves took up residence, I had to chase them away. With their spotted collars, dusky grey-pink feathers and melodious cooing the doves are prettier than their cousins the pigeons. A pair landed on my balcony and decided to set up house on the aluminium casing of the air-conditioning pipe. The casing is narrow and slippery but the doves were determined to build. It *is* a good position, high and sunny. For several days, the doves brought a selection of grass stems which they deposited on the casing and which immediately slid off. It's best to be careful around birds, to move silently so as not to alarm them. But, after observing this pair's fruitless efforts and tired of picking up stems, I loudly remonstrated with the doves, who flew off with shocked faces.

I don't mean to sentimentalise birds. Most are not gentle, placid creatures but fighters and predators, the determined defenders of their territory. Isaac Watts, the eighteenth-century preacher who coined the cloying adage 'Birds in their little nests agree', clearly had not spent much time observing them. Some species of cuckoo have a nasty habit of dumping their egg in the nest of a smaller bird. When the cuckoo chick hatches, monstrous, blind and featherless, it pushes the other eggs out of the nest, then tyrannises its adopted parents for food. Kookaburra kids often kill their brothers and sisters. Hierarchies, for some birds, are cruelly and perfunctorily administered and the punishment meted out to the young, the old or the injured can be brutal. Hens and ducks are bullies who deal with their inferiors by pecking the backs of their necks raw. A friend and I were picnicking at St Kilda's Blessington Gardens when he pointed out a gathering of white ducks with golden beaks and pristine plumage who were swaggering across the lawn, proud but comical. I noted the straggler in the flock, an isolated creature who seemed too inhibited to join the others. Its neck, tender, pink and pimpled, was denuded of feathers due to the jabs of its fellows. Its fate was sealed, I explained, and it was unlikely that the duck would ever enjoy the same companionship, food or mating rights as the others. My friend told me I'd ruined our picnic.

At Elwood Beach, I watched a silver gull turn to its neighbour dozing on the sand and, without provocation, stab its beak into the other bird's breast with all the force it could muster. Near my home, a slender canal runs through a verdant water meadow, rich with eucalypts and flowering native plants. In that little paradise, wattlebirds and mynas, magpies and mudlarks fight it out all day, sometimes it seems for the sheer pleasure of shrieking and swooping, like fighter planes, to assert who is faster, meaner, louder. Watching mynas dip and dart around my car simply for the fun of competing with its speed, I wonder if they consider cars a species of alien, ground-hugging bird. On windy days, riding the currents and tossed around the skies, birds are thrill seekers displaying the reckless confidence of the truly adept.

Magpies appear devoted parents, patiently feeding their young who, after fledging, are as large as they. The young trail the adults, wailing to be fed as they did in the nest, and the parents comply. But when the bird matures, the parents drive their child from the nesting territory with all the power their knife-sharp beaks and wicked speed allows. The magpies' glorious dawn carolling translates as little more than, 'Get the hell out of here. This place is mine.' In winter, the oval opposite my apartment hosts local football matches. The magpies, who believe the oval is theirs, stand on a tall light pole and watch with bemusement the running, yelling humans who occupy their land. After making a few half-hearted attempts to frighten them off, the magpies, outnumbered, retreat to the light pole to wait.

Birds are pragmatists. One evening in a neighbour's garden, I spotted a big sleek tabby cat, its tail twitching with anticipation, as it surveyed an unfledged magpie chick hopping about and uselessly flapping its wings. The chick had fallen from its nest somewhere nearby. Shooing away the cat, I was trying to catch the bird when, out of the blue, one of its parents descended, zooming towards the cat and me. I hoped the parent would stave off the cat so I could grab the chick. But the parent, assessing the situation after a few more swoops, disappeared into the sky. The cat, the chick and I watched its exit with decidedly different emotions. Perhaps the parent made the right decision. I managed to keep the cat at bay and capture the bird in my shopping bag. As soon as I slipped the bag over its head, it ceased struggling and squawking and lay perfectly still. Playing dead? At the vet's the next morning I was assured the bird was fine and that a wildlife officer would care for it until it was ready to be released in the wild. The young magpie had spent the night on my balcony inside a slotted laundry basket with a book for a roof. At least it had avoided a future where it would be thrashed and abandoned by its parents when they considered it old enough to fend for itself.

Cities may be inhospitable to birds but they can offer a few advantages. A different diet can change behaviour. The crows seen strutting purposefully about the streets, eating whatever they can find, are more polite than their country cousins who will pluck out the eyes of a dying lamb before feasting on its flesh. The wider array of food available in the city makes such predatory behaviour unnecessary. Some birds use our roads as maps. When the gulls that congregate in Melbourne's centre decide to head for Port Phillip Bay, they use the boulevard of St Kilda Road to navigate their route to the sea, dropping a right turn near South Melbourne. They might be heading for the banquet provided by St Kilda, a raucous, bustling, beachside tourist strip of cafes and fast food joints. (What's more raucous than a gull clamouring for food?) Or the flock could be returning to hunt in the old-fashioned way, taking from what the sea offers.

Gulls are casual builders. On a rocky promontory on Cockatoo Island in Sydney Harbour, I observed a colony of silver gulls, their nests little more than a detritus of twigs strewn on shit-spattered terrain. So completely at home were the gulls that a human leaning over the fence caused not a flicker of alarm as they attended to their chicks, brown and fluffy as sparrows. For gulls, life on the wing is obviously more attractive than labour-intensive design projects.

Birds, of course, are not the only creatures that produce nests: female alligators make holes in the damp earth in swamps to incubate their young. Termite mounds stand metres tall in the desert like weird mud-carved totems. The architecture of the beehive is a sweet, golden and humming complex. Wasps and rabbits, fish and snakes, turtles and hedgehogs make a variety of nests. Even chimpanzees construct beds from branches as night falls in their treetop residences. When it rains, they make roofs of leaves. Not all birds build nests—some move into a deserted nest built by another species, some use a ledge on a cliff.

Once upon a time, when humanity lived a more rural existence, watching birds and finding nests was an integral part of childhood. Boys, and sometimes girls, clambered up trees to examine nests and maybe to steal the eggs and the nest to boot. How can you appreciate nests if you can't see them? Where can you see them nowadays? In 2010 in the Melbourne Museum, I held a nest in my hands for the first time. It was an astonishing and exquisite experience.

The nest itself was delicate and beautiful. However, as an art historian I'm used to the regulations that govern the conservation of precious objects, whether paintings, manuscripts or photographs. The more prestigious the institution and rarer the object, the stricter the rules. I'm not arguing: collections need care. There is an etiquette involved with personally viewing or handling artworks which is rather like being seated at a formal meal. First you enter a clean, hushed, temperature-controlled room. Then a curator indicates where you will sit and offers you a pair of white cotton gloves so your grubby fingers won't stain the artwork. Then a box of treasures is placed before you. Sometimes you are not even allowed to open the lid.

When I visited the Melbourne Museum to see some of the nests, which were not on display, the young woman at the desk said, 'The nests are in there,' indicating a seminar room off the Discovery Centre. I hovered, waiting to be accompanied, to be given cotton gloves, to be shown where to sit. I had brought my own pencils for making notes. 'In *there*,' she said again, firmly but not unkindly. 'You can stay as long as you like.'

After years of obedience training, I was daunted. What if I wrecked a nest? The seminar room was unremarkable: modern, windowless, with about fifty charcoal-coloured chairs in neat rows. On the desk at the front was a huge cardboard box. I picked it up. It was light. For a moment I thought there'd been a mistake and the box was empty; then I opened it and saw it was full of nests. Each was in a snap-lock plastic bag, the sort you put sandwiches in, with a handwritten catalogue card. I slid the topmost nest out of its bag and into my hands.

The striped honeyeater's nest shimmered with long, soft, beige and tawny-coloured emu feathers, at least one hundred of them. It had been squashed flat from some previous, less commodious form of storage; otherwise it was perfectly preserved. An elaborate piece of work, it looked like an exotic purse worthy of an empress, stitched by a Surrealist seamstress. It was like holding an object that belonged to the wind and it gave the expression 'feathering your nest' quite a new meaning. Feeling my way into the lip of the nest with my fingertips, I found a dense arrangement of woven grasses. First the honeyeaters had collected the grasses and constructed the nest proper, which hangs like a hammock between the branches of a eucalypt, then they collected the feathers which they deftly slid into the interstices.

The catalogue card informed me that the nest, like many of the others in the box, had been donated by a member of the public, in this case R.P. Cooper from Milparinka in 1969. Milparinka is in a remote corner of north-western New South Wales, near the tri-borders of Queensland, New South Wales and South Australia—truly the Outback. Several parties of our doomed explorers, including Charles Sturt and Burke and Wills, trekked through the country, heading north. In the 1870s, gold was found at nearby Tibooburra, but Milparinka had something more precious in that arid region: a creek with a water hole. I learn from Penny Olsen, one of Australia's leading ornithologists, that Ray Cooper was an honorary ornithologist at the Melbourne Museum.

Emus, nomadic wanderers, congregate near water holes in the dry season. (Australia's unofficial bird emblem, the emu is a large flightless creature with a tiny head, massive feet and a voluminous feathered coat.) The honeyeaters build their nests in the same period. So the water hole at Milparinka is probably where the honeyeaters gathered the feathers that the emus had shed. Today Milparinka is a ghost town, with a population of less than 300, but emus still wander the land and perhaps the honeyeaters still gather their feathers. Did the honeyeaters use the feathers as camouflage? Emus stand up to two metres tall and honeyeaters sometimes build their nests at around the same height. Emus are big strong birds that can run like the wind and slash with their great claws. A predator, thinking it had glimpsed an emu in the brush, might desist from robbing the nest of eggs or attacking the chicks. On the other hand, Indigenous tribes avidly tracked the emus, seeking out their large eggs and often ambushing them at water holes; around Milparinka that tribe was the Maliangaapa people, who also used the water holes for their ceremonies.

The honeyeaters' nest arrived at the museum in February 1969, midsummer and the end of the breeding season. It means Ray Cooper was a nest thief, as were many of the other donors. After the honeyeaters' endeavours, they returned home to find their home was gone. Ray must have shinnied up a tree, pulled or cut the nest from its moorings and then, carefully and somewhat proudly I imagine, posted it to the museum. The catalogue card notes that the nest is unusual for its large number of feathers. Its beauty lies in its excess. This must be what enticed Cooper who, by stealing it, sought to preserve it. I slide the nest back into its plastic bag, the lustre of my pleasure somewhat dimmed. There's worse to come. The nest of the mudlark, whose official name is the Australian magpie-lark, contains three pink speckled eggs.

During one breeding season, I watched two mudlarks tend their nest in a eucalypt near the Elwood canal. They build, as their name suggests, with mud and plant fibres, on the bare horizontal fork of a tree several metres up. Prior to hatching, the couple took turns to incubate the eggs and afterwards both worked alternate shifts to feed the family. It was a dawn-to-dusk enterprise and the parent scoring the food stayed nearby in case a predator should arrive. Though I cannot know what the mudlark feels or thinks, and evolution teaches that survival is the motivating force, the uncomplaining resolve of animals is impressive, stoic and dignified. The mudlark is a quirky bird with the bold presence of its larger relative, the magpie. If I pass a mudlark when out walking along the Elwood Canal, it often won't bother to move but cocks me a sideways glance, self-contained and unafraid, with its very pale blue eyes, before continuing to forage. *It's my place too.*

In the museum, I take the mudlark's nest in my hands. The donor had thoughtfully included its foundation—a sawn-off branch. I'm surprised at how heavy it is: it must weigh around one kilo. Without a date on the catalogue card I've no clue to its age but it's rock solid and strong, without a crack, as sturdy as an ancient wall built by those other great engineers, the Romans.

Holding a nest allows you to share the bird's intimate domestic space. While the exterior of the mudlark's nest is tough, inside it's cosy and layered with grasses. The white-plumed honeyeater makes a tiny nest like a cradle, quite deep, woven with cobwebs stolen from spiders, and insulated with strands of clean white wool. The circular shape of nests is determined by their friction-built foundation—twig upon twig—or, in the case of plant fibres and mud, the shaping of moist material that dries hard. Birds don't only use their beaks to build: they press their breasts against the inner wall to make it round, imprinting their shape on their home, an interior formed by the steady rhythm of their beating hearts.

In 2010, a contemporary art exhibition in Melbourne celebrated birds. Christian Froelich, a young sculptor, made a work imitating a nest that was woven with twigs and rose brambles. Positioned aloft at the rear of the gallery, it was an arresting homage, monumental yet fragile. In a media interview, Froelich explained the difficulties of constructing the nest and how long it had taken. What if a mudlark and a magpie were invited to the gallery to assess the human's handiwork? The artist had the privilege of working at his own pace with two hands in a studio out of the weather. For birds, time is of the essence and their projects take place in nature, whatever the conditions. The magpie makes broad airy treetop nests that, cunningly, are almost indistinguishable from the branches. They may look flimsy but they are secure and Froelich's nest is not. If Froelich's nest were in a storm, the chicks would fall, and down would come baby, cradle and all.

What places Froelich's nest in the category of 'art' and excludes the birds' nests? Intent? Froelich pays tribute to birds' technical and aesthetic flair while the mudlark's goal is survival. Location? One nest is found in a gallery with a price tag attached; the other is in the wild. Design? Skill? On that count, the birds' craftsmanship is superior. Over the millennia, humans have studied avian architecture while birds—who were making homes for millions of years before homo sapiens populated the earth—learned about materials, structure, balance, endurance and disguise from the trees as well as, of course, through their own failures and successes.

The willie wagtail is a cute imp with a sharp chirruping call and it would harass a Great Dane without a second thought if the dog wandered into its territory. It's a little bird with a big personality. Found all over Australia, it has a distinctive dance, hopping along the ground and wiggling its black iridescent tail. In Aboriginal mythology, the willie wagtail is associated with gossip and deviousness in social relationships. Don't say anything in confidence if there's a wagtail around! Its mud nest is tiny, about seven millimetres across, ringed with cobwebs and leaves. In the museum, I hold it in the palm of my hand. How does a family of six fit? The parents must sit on top of the youngsters, shielding them from the elements and keeping them warm. Inside it's cushioned and springy like a miniature mattress. Birds keep their nests scrupulously clean. Helpfully, the nestlings' poo comes in a faecal sac that the parents carry away, an activity almost as time-consuming as finding food and feeding their babies. When the nestlings get older, they hang their little behinds over the nest edge. The birds who don't have poo bags, like pigeons, have very smelly nests indeed.

The wagtail's nest was found in 1952, so it's the same vintage as me. Growing older, I've learned to appreciate birds. Perhaps it's the humility that comes with age and which recognises that the struggle for existence—Charles Darwin's phrase—is shared by us all. Issues about hierarchies in nature, who is the boss of whom, seem less compelling at this point in the planet's history than what we can learn from one another, whatever our species. Birds, with their capacity for building their homes unaided—quite aside from their ability to fly and to inspire us to do the same—should earn our respect as they manage to make the trials of life look graceful.

In the 1980s, I began visiting Apollo Bay, regularly spending part of each year there, and that's where I began watching birds. There are two equally intriguing ways to get to the bay: the first is along the winding and aptly named Great Ocean Road, the second is the quicker route through the massive forests of the Otway Ranges. In winter, if you're lucky, it will be snowing in the mountains. It was my friend Stephen Benwell who introduced me to Apollo Bay and who showed me the bowerbird.

With his wide amber eyes and slender frame, Stephen is as handsome and amusing as a cat. He made an ideal travelling companion. Stephen can seem casual, even lazy, but he is a practical person. He'd been a scout during his miserable years at one of Melbourne's classiest boys' schools. His father went there so he did too, though for a young gay man in the 1960s it had little to offer. Then he attended art school, like his mother, and became a potter who paints watercolours on clay, floating transparent figures on giant irregular vases, little statues of vanilla-coloured men who appear to be melting, and small fantastic animals.

An expert navigator, Stephen took the wheel in a most gentlemanly fashion on our travels and kept a stash of maps in the glovebox. When I went to New Mexico, he loaned me the map he had used twenty years before. He explained that, to reach my destination at Ghost Ranch in the desert beyond Santa Fe, I had to drive due north for about an hour until I reached Espanola, then I turned left and that was the only turn I had to make until I reached the entrance for Ghost Ranch. I was terrified of driving in America, something I had never done, let alone through a desert. I felt so frightened I couldn't imagine it, as if my mind had shut down and just wouldn't let me think. But when I got into the rented car and timidly headed out of Santa Fe, I put the map on the seat next to me, Stephen's map, and knew I'd find my way.

On our journey to Apollo Bay, Stephen and I stopped at Wye River on the Great Ocean Road. Strewn under a bush, I noticed a collection of small, bright blue objects—glass, buttons, feathers. I wondered if it was rubbish dumped by whoever had been there before us; odd that it was all the same colour. Stephen explained it was the work of a bird—a satin bowerbird—and if we waited the bird would return. The male bowerbird doesn't make a nest but a bower, a spectacular and studied creation.

Shortly afterwards there was bustling in the undergrowth and a medium-sized, black-feathered bird appeared with a shard of blue plastic in his beak. He placed it with the other objects, inspected the arrangement, made a few adjustments and then flew off. But that's not all. Behind this colour-coded display, the male builds a bower, a symmetrical twig arcade which he daubs with pulped fruit and saliva, often applied with a wad of bark fibres like a paintbrush held in his beak. This is the inner sanctum where he will mate with a female—if she so desires. That's what all this activity is about: seduction. 'Painting' the arcade is also designed to please the female: not only does it subtly hue the bower, it also provides something for her to snack on while she judges the male's presentation, and watches him sing and dance. Often, after the male's complex and frantic display, the female flies off, unimpressed. Sometimes she needs to hide in the bower because the revved-up male can go berserk and attack her.

Scientists are fascinated by bowerbirds because they clearly demonstrate the power of sexual selection, the evolutionary force that Darwin defined to explain conspicuous male traits such as song, bright colours, and horns. In *The Descent of Man*, Darwin made particular note of the male bowerbird's display: 'The playing passages of bower-birds are tastefully ornamented with gaily-coloured objects; and this shews that they must receive some sort of pleasure from the sight of such things.'[2] As writer Virginia Morell notes, these multi-talented birds can

> build a hut that looks like a doll's house; they can arrange flowers, leaves and mushrooms in such an artistic manner you'd be forgiven for thinking that Matisse was about to set up his easel; some can sing simultaneously both the male and female parts of another species' duet, and others easily imitate the raucous laugh of a kookaburra or the roar of a chainsaw. Plus, they all dance.[3]

Satin bowerbirds opt for a blue palette with a few hints of yellow, while in the tropical woodlands of northern Australia the great bowerbird selects a fashionably muted range of orna-ments—bleached snail shells, stones and pebbles, sometimes adding a note or two of olive-green for contrast. It might even choose only one object and one hue, such as uniformly sized grey stones, to create a dramatic, minimalist Zen-like effect. The male's 'welcome mats' can include thousands of items, sometimes filched from other males competing nearby for the female's attention. In New Guinea, the Macgregor's bowerbird may spend weeks erecting, and years perfecting, a 'maypole' bower up to two metres high atop a ring of moss. Others, like the Vogelkop, also found in New Guinea, make patterns with hot-pink flowers, black beans and wide green leaves on the jungle floor. Human rubbish is not ignored and the enterprising Vogelkops collect discarded soft-drink cans and brightly coloured confectionery bags to lure the female. Indeed, Western researchers believed for decades that the bowers must be the work of diminutive undiscovered forest tribes.

Scientists are wary of anthropomorphism, the assignment of human characteristics to animals. As naturalist and author Lyanda Lynn Haupt comments, most young scientists take their first university classes under a sign that actually forbids it. At her college the sign read 'Thou Shalt Not Anthropomorphize', and it was 'penned in ornamental calligraphy on faux parchment, as if it had been inscribed by a medieval monk taking dictation directly from God'.[4] Anecdotal observation is also frowned upon. As you are already aware, this book is full of such crimes. In Darwin's time, however, when the professions of 'scientist' and 'ornithologist' were being defined, anthropomorphism was not viewed with the same opprobrium with which current scientists regard it. Darwin's sympathetic participation with animals—which makes his writings about birds, for example, so engaging—was quite common. In the Falkland Islands, Darwin spotted carrion hawks which he described as 'very mischievous and inquisitive . . . [they] are quarrelsome, and extremely passionate; it was curious to behold them when, impatient, tearing up the grass with their bills from rage'.[5] Petrels approaching his ship were 'tame & sociable, & silent' and a certain thrush especially 'inquisitive'.[6] Haupt describes how Darwin 'utterly, and even joyfully, abandoned his privileged human status. He threw his own thoughts and behaviours right into the animal mix, putting all creatures, including humans, on the same continuum of consciousness.' It meant that rather than imposing human consciousness upon animal behaviours, Darwin 'animalized consciousness in general'.[7]

Recently Mike Hansell, emeritus professor at the University of Glasgow and an expert on animal architecture, has become emboldened to believe that 'not only might bowerbirds feel pleasure from building the bower but also that we might be able to obtain objective evidence of it'.[8] The bowerbird's skill at designing fabulous colour schemes and extravagant bowers develops over several years, and the more sophisticated the bower, the better the bird's success rate in attracting a female. It seems that males and females recognise and enjoy 'a sense of beauty', as Darwin described it.[9] What the bowerbird admires, so do we. Aghast at his temerity, Hansell wonders if he seems to be 'losing his critical faculties in suggesting that bowerbirds might be artists'.[10] After all, the study of animal behaviour needs to show objectivity and investigate only the measurable to establish its scientific credentials. But

Darwin's preparedness to use his imagination has encouraged a discerning and influential scientist like Hansell to consider that some non-human animals, such as the bowerbird, have a capacity for discriminating visual pleasure. Does the female bowerbird fall in love with a beautiful mind?

At the museum, the female satin bowerbird's nest was the oldest in the box. It was found on 10 February 1900 by S.W. Jackson near the Bellinger River in New South Wales, half a metre from the ground. According to its accompanying note, it was in 'an Oak tree near the edge of a dense Cedar scrub'. After mating, the male and female have no further contact and the female raises the family alone, not unusual in the animal world. After the intense scrutiny to which she subjects the male's creation, the female doesn't waste her time on ornaments and bravura technique, though her nest is lovely in its simplicity.

I watched a documentary that showed a bowerbird busily arranging the boudoir. When he'd nearly finished, a brush turkey many times larger than he wandered through the bower searching for food, picking and kicking his way along the forest floor. The bowerbird, forced to sit to one side and watch the methodical disarray of his composition, seethed. *Philistine.* Perhaps one artist in the family is enough.

2
Picturing nests

I DISCOVERED DARWIN THE HARD way. It was 1965 and in my Bible studies class at Catholic Ladies College we were reading a commentary on Genesis. Sister Anthony was the class teacher, a tall, stooped, gaunt woman whose deathly pallor was emphasised by her floor-length black robes. Her face and hands were the only parts of her body visible. Around her neck she wore a gleaming crucifix with which she played, and from her waist swung long wooden rosary beads and an impressive bunch of keys. She seemed ancient. Sister Anthony did not walk into the classroom with the rest of us but emerged from behind a door that led to the mysterious, forbidden realm of the convent. This apparition each morning was sensational, theatrical and made us quiet. We were scared of

Sister Anthony. She forced us to pin our hair back from our faces, every strand, and she kept a supply of bobby pins in her desk for that purpose. If we were unable to complete the strict coiffure to her satisfaction, she did it for us, roughly with cold fingers. She had a walking stick, and if her temper was up she'd use it to strike out at us. But, so frail, she rarely moved from the vantage point of her desk so we learned to keep our distance and, if she attempted to lure us close for chastisement, to dart away.

Sister Anthony seemed so unearthly that when she once tripped and fell in the playground, we little girls dared not touch her, help her, raise her but stared in paralysed silence until another nun came to her rescue. I have friends who attended Catholic schools who become sentimental when they recall the nuns from their childhood, wise, kind-hearted women who counselled and encouraged their students. Unfortunately I did not meet such nuns.

Bible studies was tedious and so was the commentary on Genesis and my mind dawdled until I saw the footnote: 'The evolution hypothesis, which proposes that man is descended from the apes, is not accepted by the Catholic Church.' *Apes*, I thought. *How cool.* I can't recall the book I found at the local library later that week that explained Darwin's ideas but I became an immediate and passionate believer in evolution. It seemed God *should* be capable of such subtlety, complexity and invention. Why get the creation of the world over in six days when allowing it to evolve over millions of years offered a far more entertaining process? Also, the prospect of being related to animals seemed, to an imaginative child, as enchanting as a fairytale where a girl could chat with a wolf or dine with bears. Imbued with the ardour of the newly converted, I rushed into class and announced to Sister Anthony, 'Darwin was right! We're descended from the apes!' I'm not sure what I expected to happen next. That Sister Anthony would see the light, shout hallelujah and embrace me? She replied, with icy fury, that believing in evolution was a mortal sin and I must go immediately to confession and receive penance otherwise I would burn in the flames of hell forever. She was quite perceptive. Two years later, I was expelled.

Darwin was a self-effacing, brave and sickly man who took years to muster the courage to publish his views in *On the Origin of Species*. It was a painful saga incorporating self-doubt, constant and undiagnosed ailments, and the slow death of his adored child Annie. The struggle for Darwin to produce *Origin of Species* and the repercussions of its publication were captured in a number of books and films that celebrated, in 2009, the two hundredth anniversary of Darwin's birth and the hundred and fiftieth anniversary of the publication of *Origin of Species*. They include, most notably, Jon Amiel's feature film *Creation*, based on the book

Annie's Box by Darwin's great-great-grandson Randal Keynes; *Darwin's Brave New World*, a three-part TV dramatisation; and Richard Dawkins' book *The Greatest Show on Earth: The evidence for evolution*. I feel grateful to Darwin—not for setting me on the course that got me kicked out of school, but for being the first important voice to suggest that birds have an aesthetic sense. He lends a degree of scientific credence to the idea I'm exploring in this book, which some readers may find whimsical or even bizarre.

Darwin's five-year odyssey as a young man on HMS *Beagle* gave him the opportunity to study wild nature in South America, Australia, New Zealand, South Africa and the seas and islands in between. Though Darwin writes that he joined the *Beagle* 'as naturalist', in fact he was invited to make the voyage as the dining companion of Captain FitzRoy, the ship's master and commander. A diplomatic role, Darwin's job was to entertain the noble but temperamental FitzRoy, and the affectionate bond that grew between the men indicates how well Darwin acquitted his task.

When Darwin set off on the *Beagle* in 1831 he may have been an obsessive beetle hunter but he was not a naturalist. At twenty-two, he was something of a wastrel and the despair of his father Robert, a physician with the imposing personality of the nineteenth-century patriarch. Young Darwin had fled the operating theatre of Edinburgh University, where Robert had wished him to train as a doctor, because he found the sights and sounds of an operation performed on a child without anaesthetic too hideous to bear. Darwin preferred to dally rather than to study: his preferred occupations were shooting, hunting and rambling about the countryside. Darwin senior regarded his son's travel plans with dismay and initially rejected them. But Charles was canny enough to realise that family money meant he did not need to pursue a conventional career and could indulge his fancies. By the time the *Beagle* returned to England, Darwin had emerged as a superbly gifted naturalist.

While Darwin's writing about nature was lucid and engaging, he was hampered by a lack of talent in another area: he could not draw. So when he decided to publish and edit the sumptuous five-volume *Zoology of the Voyage of HMS* Beagle, he needed an artist's vision to illustrate the rare creatures he'd found. Though Darwin gained both public and private funding for the costly long-term enterprise, it was not enough, so he buttressed the venture with his own cash. For the volume on birds, part three of the series that was published between 1838 and 1841, Darwin employed the services of John and Elizabeth Gould. Darwin was most fortunate in his choice: not only was Elizabeth one of the best bird artists of any era, but John's authoritative and encyclopaedic knowledge of birds would help Darwin to make his name.

The bird-mad Gould had lowly beginnings. His father was a gardener who in 1818 became foreman of the Royal Gardens of Windsor, today known as Windsor Great Park. John was then fourteen and the park became his playground and his university, giving him the chance to advance his appetite for knowledge of the natural world. By the time he was twenty-three, Gould had established a successful taxidermy business and he was appointed to the prestigious post of curator and preserver at the museum of the Zoological Society of London.

Perhaps it's not surprising that Gould's favourite species was the hummingbird: clear parallels can be drawn between those tireless, darting avian perfectionists whose speed is so intense it can escape the human eye and Gould's relentless and fastidious exploration of birds, which in his case resulted in a prodigious number of top quality publications. Birds make nests quickly and Gould produced books with alacrity. That other great nineteenth-century ornithologist John James Audubon was similarly obsessed, admitting that he felt an intimacy with birds that bordered on frenzy. When Audubon visited England in 1826 to raise money to publish his masterpiece *The Birds of America*, the public couldn't get enough of the American woodsman. Even George IV became a fan. Darwin, then a student, heard Audubon lecture on how to display stuffed birds in a lifelike way. Later, he quoted

Audubon in *Origin of Species*. Meanwhile, Audubon's success set an example Gould clearly wished to best.

When Darwin presented the mammal and bird specimens he'd collected during the *Beagle* voyage to the Geological Society of London at their meeting on 4 January 1837, the birds were given to Gould for identification. It took Gould less than a week to make a remarkable discovery. Birds that Darwin had brought back from the Galápagos Islands which he had thought were blackbirds and 'Gross-beaks' were, Gould announced, 'a series of ground Finches which are so peculiar' as to form 'an entirely new group, containing 12 species', unique to the Galápagos.[1] The story made the newspapers. In March 1837, Darwin attended a lecture by Gould at the Zoological Society where he discussed the South American 'ostrich' that Darwin had brought back. The specimen had sufficient differences from other ostriches to consider it a separate species which Gould magnanimously named *Rhea darwinii*. Darwin mulled over Gould's conclusions. Isolated on the Galápagos, it seemed the finches had evolved separately, which was why they were neither blackbirds nor grosbeaks, as Darwin had first thought. The *Rhea darwinii* was not an ostrich but its physical resemblance to an ostrich made it hard to ignore the possibility of a common ancestry. For Darwin it proved a crucial passage in the theory of evolution by natural selection, and Gould had drawn his attention to it. Could every creature, whenever and wherever they had lived on earth, be connected? Could everything, humankind included, be part of one ancestral chain?

In 1829, Gould had married Elizabeth Coxen, known as Eliza. Legend has it they met at London Zoo where Eliza was sketching. At twenty-five, she was a talented artist who was eager to escape her humdrum job as a governess. Gould's observations are acutely perceptive but, like Darwin, his sketches of birds are clumsy and rudimentary. John encouraged his wife to learn lithography from the artist and poet Edward Lear, who was in his employ. The print medium of lithography rivalled painting in its exactitude. Eliza didn't merely transfer Gould's sketches to the lithographer's stone, she also transformed them into exceptional illustrations. Gould's publications were expensive and available only to a limited clientele. Nonetheless, they made possible the wider dissemination of knowledge about birds and their nests. John and Eliza were a formidable team: Gould wrote about birds with a contagious and endearing sense of wonder while Eliza conveyed the birds' personalities, especially in the treatment of their eyes—alert and shining with life—and endowed their plumage with a lustrous, tactile quality. Darwin was thrilled with the results. For *Zoology of the Voyage of HMS* Beagle, Mrs Gould had executed the drawings in stone 'with that admirable success which has attended all her works'.[2]

In 1838, the Goulds sailed to Tasmania to begin a most ambitious project. *The Birds of Australia*, published between 1840 and 1848, comprises seven volumes that include 600 impeccably accurate life-size plates. It remains the most comprehensive work produced on the subject. The Goulds' illustrations were groundbreaking, the first time that many species and their nests had been seen. The satin bowerbird received a double-page spread. Gould could not help boasting that 'although this species has been known to ornithologists . . . its habits, [*sic*] which in many respects are quite extraordinary, have hitherto escaped attention; or if not entirely so, have never been brought before the scientific world. It is, therefore, a source of high gratification to myself to be the first to place them on record.'[3] As well as depicting the bower, the Goulds included a display of four different birds: an adult male and female, an aged male bowerbird with its variegated green and blue feathers, and a younger male before it assumed its iridescent plumage. Gould was a punctilious collector. Not content to record the bower, he shipped back to London every twig and ornament from four complete bowers. When they were put on display at the Zoological Society, they caused quite a stir.

The Goulds were based in Hobart, where they were befriended by the governor Sir John Franklin and his wife, Jane. Eliza did not choose to accompany John on his specimen-collecting treks: she was pregnant for part of their stay and afterwards nursed their son, who was named Franklin for their friends. The Goulds' eldest child, Henry, had accompanied his parents to Tasmania, while Charles, Eliza and Louisa, who were too young for the long sea voyage, had remained in England where they were cared for by their grandmother. During Gould's absences Eliza found amusement and employment in drawing plants 'which will help render the work on Birds of Australia more interesting'. She was highly praised for her work. 'I wish you could hear some of the magnificent speeches,' she wrote to her mother. But Eliza missed her children and longed to be in 'dear dear' England.[4]

The Birds of Australia is not merely a compendium of species, it is also a homage to birds, a romance about nature, a combination of rapturous writing and immaculately attentive imagery. The white-shafted fantail, Gould notes, has an

> elegant little nest, closely resembling a wine-glass in shape . . . woven together with exquisite skill, and is generally composed of the inner bark of a species of *Eucalyptus*, neatly lined with the down of the tree-fern intermingled with flowering stalks of moss, and outwardly matted together with the webs of spiders, which not only serve to envelop the nest, but are also employed to strengthen its attachment to the branch on which it is constructed.[5]

Gould was astonished by the mudlark's nest, which resembled 'a massive clay-coloured earthenware vessel' and which may be regarded as 'one of the anomalies of Australia, so unlike is it to anything usually met with'.[6] Gould was appalled by the treatment of Aboriginal people by the colonists. Indigenous tribes revered birds and knew their lore, treating them as part of a harmonious spiritual universe, and Gould learned from native people. When he could, he included the Aboriginal names for birds in *The Birds of Australia*.

Until the advent of photography, death and ornithology went hand in hand. Live birds could be observed in their native habitat, but to study them in detail they had to be dead. Darwin and Gould were excellent marksmen who could bring down their prey using fine shot and causing a minimum of damage. Not long after the Goulds' arrival in Tasmania, Eliza wrote to her mother that John had 'already shown himself a great enemy to the feathered tribe, having shot a great many beautiful birds and robbed various others of their nests and eggs. Indeed John is so enthusiastic that one cannot be with him without catching some of his zeal.'[7]

Both Darwin and Gould were taxidermists, another talent necessary to the study of wild things in that era. Now as then, taxidermy is a messy business. The bird is sliced open with a scalpel, then the skin is methodically separated from the innards, the eyes and the brain drained. The remainder of the body is discarded. Leaving the skull and legs in place, the skin is gently shrugged over the shoulders, before being stuffed with cottonwool, straw or wads of hemp, and then carefully sewn back together. In those days, arsenic was used as a preservative, though moths and other bugs sometimes chewed their way in regardless, turning many specimens into rotten lumpy heaps. Eye sockets were filled with cotton, making the expressive eyes that Eliza gave her studies particularly noteworthy because she had to imagine them. Bird fanciers in the field sometimes did not stuff their prey, merely relieved them of their insides, because the process of taxidermy was so arduous. Darwin brought back thousands of dead creatures from his journey on the *Beagle* and did not have time and space to thoroughly preserve them all.

Taxidermy became a fad in mid-Victorian Britain which, like the rest of Europe, craved novelties from the natural world. For sportsmen it offered the chance to display their kill and boast of their exploits, the victory of mankind over nature. However, taxidermy gradually gained scientific importance as the specimens became valuable objects of research. Visitors to museums and private collections could now view hitherto-unknown species. It was Gould who led the field in the preservation of birds and who helped to give the nascent science of ornithology its status.

Taxidermy led to the creation of dioramas, the theatrical three-dimensional displays that became popular in museums. Carl Akeley made the first complete museum habitat diorama for the Milwaukee Museum in 1890. Like Gould, Akeley didn't bother much with a conventional education and attended school for a few scant years before committing himself to taxidermy, travel, wild animals and the construction of increasingly elaborate dioramas. His effort for New York's American Museum of Natural History remains on display. In 1921, Akeley went to the Congo to hunt gorillas destined for a diorama but, humbled by his encounter with the great apes on Mount Mikeno in the Virunga range, he became a conservationist, committed to preserving the gorillas in their habitat rather than in a museum.

The Birds of Australia was a great success but it proved to be Gould's work of mourning. Eliza died in 1841, shortly after the birth of a daughter, and Gould completed the enterprise with other illustrators, including Henry Constantine Richter, William Matthew Hart and Joseph Wolf. Some say Gould worked Eliza to death—manically energetic himself, he was a hard taskmaster—and her reputation was completely eclipsed by his. A painting of Eliza, completed in memoriam by an unknown artist, shows her holding a cockatiel, *Nymphicus hollandicus*, a relative of the budgerigar. Eliza has a long, intelligent, rather sad face, with gentle, dark brown eyes and full, nearly smiling lips. A single glossy brown curl droops over her forehead. The rendering of the cockatiel is far below Eliza's own standards and looks, as it no doubt was, stuffed. Eliza was an unwilling nymph of New Holland (the historic name for Australia given by the Dutch seafarer Abel Tasman), who had to leave behind England and her brood for its shores. Like the birds her husband captured, Eliza, too, was trapped by his obsessions.

•

It was during the summers spent at Apollo Bay that I realised how little I knew about birds, especially the varieties along that coast. With Stephen, I'd gone walking in the forest where I spied my first fairy wren. In summer, for the ladies, the male wears a stunning costume. I'll let John Gould describe: the male undergoes

> a total transformation, not only in colour, but also in the texture of its plumage; indeed a more astonishing change can scarcely be imagined, its plain and unassuming garb being thrown off for a few months and another assumed, for which its resplendent beauty is hardly surpassed by any of the feathered race . . . nor is the change confined to plumage alone but extends to its habits, in fact, its whole character and nature appear to have received a new impulse; the little

creature now displaying great vitality, proudly showing off its gorgeous plumage to the utmost advantage and pouring out animated song unceasingly.[8]

Watching the male wren in the shadows of the forest was like watching a brilliant, dancing, blue light.

While as a child I admired illustrations of birds, such images stank of death. Their verisimilitude, their awful stillness was eerie. Nature programs on television were educative but the images lasted only an instant. Birds are secretive and few species wish any to see their nests, which are meant to be either invisible or unreachable.

In the Melbourne Museum, I saw my first blackbird's nest. Blackbirds themselves are ubiquitous: I must have seen hundreds throughout Europe and in southern Australia where they were introduced in the nineteenth century. But I'd never so much as glimpsed a nest. They're noticeable birds, noisily picking their way through leaf litter, assessing humans with a quick, smart glance and giving a piercing trill—a warning to their mate—as they fly off. Because the birds are so common, I expected their nests to be casual, something of a shambles like the silver gulls' nests I saw on Cockatoo Island. But the females make a sturdy yet supple—and by no means inelegant—arrangement of grasses woven with fine twigs. The males help with feeding the young, and during the breeding season sing at evening, an intense, melodious, captivating song. Sitting at my desk, early in spring, I can hear the blackbird as night falls and work ends for the day, his song accompanying me, counterpointing my domestic rhythms as I switch off the computer and leave the study, move through the flat turning on lights, pour myself a glass of wine and begin to unwind, to plan the night ahead.

The birds we see around us don't make many mistakes. That's because the foolish ones who didn't manage to do the job properly were bred out by natural selection. Like us, the birds are winners, survivors of the struggle for existence. But because of us many species are extinct and others continue to decline. Nature is not beyond us, outside, out there; nature *is* us.

Photography changed our perception of nature because it captured animals without killing or caging them. Painting has traditionally 'staged' animals, encoding them within human narratives. In the history of Western art, birds don't tell their own stories but act as moral representatives of ours. Goya's *Don Manuel Osorio Manrique de Zuñiga* (c. 1784–1792, Metropolitan Museum of Art, New York) is a portrait of the son of the count and countess Altamira, members of a wealthy banking family in Madrid. A beautiful child dressed in his best, Manuel is radiantly innocent. On a string, he holds a live magpie, his plaything, which, in its beak, holds a card inscribed with Goya's signature. In the shadows, three cats with burning eyes watch the magpie fixedly while the child, staring outwards, is oblivious to nature's cruel game. Innocence will be destroyed, Goya comments, and perhaps freedom and culture, too. The bird carries the artist's name and, in the darkness, the forces of violence and unreason gather to destroy it.

Goya enjoyed a stellar career as court painter to the Spanish royal family. But, from 1774 to 1784, Goya and his wife Josefa had shared the tragic experience of watching six of their seven children die in either childbirth or early infancy. During the 1790s, in response to the brutality and paranoia generated by the Spanish Inquisition, and his own deepening pessimism, Goya worked on *Los Caprichos*. It's a series of eighty etchings that depict, like hideous nightmares, animals and humankind as equally demented and sadistic. The best known is *The Sleep of Reason Produces Monsters*. Perhaps it's no wonder that Don Manuel glows with an unearthly luminosity while in the shadows, savagery and death wait.

Eadweard Muybridge was the revolutionary English photographer based in America who freeze-framed the movements of humans and animals by using an extremely fast shutter speed and multiple cameras. His book *Animal Locomotion*, published in 1887, caused a sensation because it disproved the way the human eye had read any number of actions from the canter of a horse to the flight of a bird. Until *Animal*

Locomotion there hadn't been the opportunity to observe in detail how the bodies of humans and animals worked. Artists and scientists were equally fascinated by Muybridge's results. He photographed men, women and a variety of animals, including a hawk, vulture, ostrich, eagle, stork and swan. For the first time, the mechanics of a bird in flight could be scrutinised. Muybridge was a landscape photographer who'd attracted attention for his photographs of Yosemite National Park, and perhaps the acute observation he practised in nature made Muybridge determined to understand every aspect of natural movement. His approach was egalitarian: humans, birds and beasts were subjected to the same photographic process and observed with similar dispassion.

The *Reader's Digest Complete Book of Australian Birds* is a large book I've lugged to Apollo Bay time and again. It's how I learned that I'd spotted a superb fairy wren or a sooty oyster catcher, a goshawk or a falcon. One of its most dramatic and instructive features is that many photographs were taken as birds alight at their nests. A kestrel arrives with a mouse in her beak while a gaggle of squawking, open-mouthed chicks nearly fall from the nest with excitement. The Forest Kingfisher, a dragonfly clamped firmly in her bill, enters a termite mound that she and her partner have excavated for their brood. Three barn owls with enormous eyes and lustrous white-feathered faces peer inquisitively at the camera from their home in a tree hole. The Southern Fulmar, a large seabird whose empire is the Southern Ocean, shrieks from its nest in a rocky crevice, warning the interloper behind the camera he might get a sharp peck.

Wildlife photographer Andy Rouse used an attacking bird to get a memorable shot. On a bleak afternoon in Antarctica with a lowering sky, he was returning from photographing a penguin colony when he wandered into territory occupied by nesting skuas. The skuas are unassailable. Loud, violent pirates and scavengers who steal eggs from penguins, force smaller birds to disgorge their food and squabble madly among themselves, they have no fear of humans. As a skua attacked Rouse, beak open, wings spread, he used the camera to fend off the bird and to photograph it at the same time. The result is a wonderfully scary moment, the picture of a hostile creature in an equally hostile terrain.

Having made a few clumsy attempts to photograph birds, I am full of admiration for the patience, skill and nerve displayed by those who can (beautifully) record a bird and its nest. The fairy terns were a case in point. Gould was so taken by Darwin's description of the tern, he quoted it in *The Birds of Australia*:

There is one charming bird: a small and snow-white Tern which smoothly hovers at the distance of an arm's length from your head; its large black eye scanning with quiet curiosity your expression. Little imagination is required to fancy that so light and delicate a body must be tenanted by some wandering fairy spirit.[9]

On a remote beach in Victoria, I saw a flock of terns asleep on the sand. They were resting on their migration from Tasmania to Australia's north-west coast, far, far away. So finely built, they looked like origami; in flight, their brilliant wings seem translucent. To feed, terns plunge-dive into the sea—that is, they don't fully compress their wings. It makes for a startling sight as the tiny creatures smash through the surface of the water with a force that seems unsuitable for such frail bodies. But after each dive the terns calmly arose with fish in their bills. Sadly, my photographs showed a pale haze on the sand and when the terns were in flight, a blur.

Sharon Beals is a nature photographer based in San Francisco who makes what she calls 'nest portraits'.[10] It was a project that started almost by chance when a friend brought Beals an abandoned nest and, intrigued, she sought to capture its intricacy. Using a high-resolution flatbed scanner she made images of the nest. But she faced two problems. Firstly, after turning the nest upside down on the scanner, she had to spend hours cleaning the dust that falls from the nests off the images in Photoshop. Secondly, possessing nests is illegal.

Beals overcame the technical challenge by using high-resolution cameras and by taking multiple exposures, focusing on different planes and then blending the images. The legal issue was more tricky. Like Australia, the United States has very strict laws governing protected species, as I learned when I discovered a dead mudlark on the Elwood Canal. It must have been a split-second thing: the bird's attention was momentarily distracted and it crashed into the bank, breaking its neck. It was a weird sight because the bird had hit the ground with such impact that its body was perpendicular to the earth. When I reached it, it was still warm and, aside from its neck, undamaged. Gently, I carried the mudlark home and laid it on the table on the balcony. Does it sound ghoulish to say I'd hoped to get it stuffed? But the taxidermist I contacted explained it was illegal, and the Department of Sustainability and Environment concurred. If I'd found a pigeon or a myna, it would be sitting preserved on a shelf in my living room. I was also advised that if I'd already collected any native specimens from the wild, even roadkill, they should either be destroyed—burning or burial were the suggested options—or handed in to the department for disposal. All native birds are protected. The mudlark became landfill.

Of course, I support the laws. Staying in Tuscany some years ago, I witnessed a ritual practised by some of the local men. Kitted out in full camouflage gear, rifles at the ready, a dozen or so would spend their Saturday afternoons in the valley below the house where I was staying, blasting every living thing they could find, accompanied by dogs. The prize was pathetic. After all, it was Tuscany in the late twentieth century, there was virtually nothing left to hunt, so their game were tiny gold-green finches no bigger than your thumb. Today, perhaps even those birds have been decimated.

Beals countered the legal issue of possessing nests by photographing the past. She visited the California Academy of Sciences and the Museum of Vertebrate Zoology at Berkeley to study nests that had been collected decades ago and which continue to provide valuable scientific data. It's interesting that while birds are profligate about their architecture, often discarding it after one breeding season, the nests themselves can be so well made that, if properly stored, they last indefinitely. Beals was delighted with the range of nests available to her and their aesthetic potential: 'I loved the quiet, subdued palette, and the shapes created by the form-follows-function of the nest builders themselves. I loved the amazing variety of content and construction, the way the materials became like line and brushstroke.'[11] She began printing the images larger than life, on sheets of fine etching paper. The results are opulent and intimate, the images crisply defined and richly glowing. Beals shoots against a black ground, spotlighting the nest and centralising it, personalising the object so it becomes a new kind of subject. Often she shoots from above, opening the nest to the viewer's gaze.

The pine siskin is native to North America and is Washington state's most populous bird. It's a communal little creature, about thirteen centimetres in length, and the flock inhabits a maple tree and builds their nests close together. Beals' photograph shows the nest encased within a nest, the dried leaves of the maple which the pine siskin has chosen to act as both camouflage from predators and protection from the elements. Within this autumn-hued double embrace three white eggs are seen, the still point of a swirling, centrifugal composition. The word 'nest' conjures fundamental notions of home, family, privacy, shelter and rest. It's a word of embrace, of origins, both visceral and tender. Beals' photograph under-scores the metaphor.

I have a crush on Sir David Attenborough and have fantasies about going on adventures with him. Not only is he handsome with an irrepressible enthusiasm and a gallant charm, he can make the most intricate aspects of animal behaviour as digestible as an after-dinner chat. He is light-footed in rough terrain and I'm sure he would make an excellent partner on the dance floor were we to take a spin. For years, he's been my teacher about nature.

In one of my fantasies, he rescues me. (He is a knight, after all.) I'm in Namibia to visit the sociable weavers. These plain little birds that resemble sparrows don't just make nests, they construct permanent, multi-level apartment buildings. After choosing an isolated tree, the large weaver community, which may number two or three hundred, collects grasses and builds around one hundred straw chambers using different materials for different purposes. They make a tough, waterproof outer skin; inside they embroider their havens with flowers and soft grasses. Each family has a self-contained unit with its own downward-pointing entrance. The result looks like a gigantic drooping hay bale designed by Salvador Dalí.

In my fantasy, I'm with a group of tourists on safari in the Kalahari Desert. Bored with the slowness of the expedition and eager to find the weavers, I wander off, something I'm inclined to do and which has got me into trouble more than once. As night falls, I realise I'm lost and feel stupid and very scared. In the Kalahari, temperatures can drop to minus seven or eight degrees Celsius overnight and, lightly clad, I'm ill-equipped for such contingencies. I'm also in a place where creatures much bigger than myself hunt at night. I consider the possibility of being chased by a lion. Could I climb a tree and seek refuge? Perhaps a weavers' tree? Other animals are attracted to the weavers' five-star accommodation. Lovebirds, tits and finches sleep in the spare rooms. Vultures, owls, eagles and even geese find the nest roof a reliable platform from which to land or take off. On the other hand, it's not entirely safe. Cobras haunt the branches for prey so the weavers rim their nests with sharp straw spikes to deter enemies. I find myself wondering if lions kill quickly. They do in the TV programs I've watched.

Suddenly, a convoy of four-wheel drives comes racing across the desert, headlights cutting through the darkness. It brakes, coming to a halt a few metres from me.

'Good lord,' says Sir David, stepping nimbly from the first car. 'What are you doing out here?' It's a question asked so affably and courteously that it stops me from bursting into tears with relief.

'I'm after the weavers.' I try for a measured, casual tone.

'Well, so are we,' says Sir David in delighted surprise. 'You must come along with us and we'll find them together.'

As the BBC camera crew unpack their gear, I follow Sir David across the desert. He doesn't make me feel like a fool by asking how on earth I managed to get lost in the African wilderness. Rather, he explains how the weavers insulate their nests so it's always comfortable inside whatever the external temperature.

'Here we are,' he says, shining his torch into a tree with wide overhanging branches. It's like looking into a treetop honeycomb, a coral reef in the air. Hundreds of little faces peer back, unafraid, merely interested in the visitors. 'They're in *bed*,' Sir David explains in his gently emphatic way. 'They've been out hunting all day and they've just arrived home. Good *timing*.' He beams at me. Together we observe the nest until the crew arrives. Sir David is a pro and needs only a few takes. Then the guides who accompany the crew make a fire and we sit around, sipping an excellent red, as Sir David regales us with tales of his adventures.

The Life of Birds, presented by Attenborough in 1998, was a ten-part TV series that saw him globe-hopping from the Galápagos to Alaska to Lapland to Florida. Of all the remarkable birds that he and his crew captured on film, the nest of the golden-headed cisticola ranks highly. Even Sir David, who is not given to hyperbole, was gobsmacked, stating that: 'There is no more skilled tailor in the whole of the bird world.' The bird, native to wetlands from South-east Asia to Australia, literally sews its nest together. The female collects plant fibres and spiderwebs that it uses not just for lining its tiny nest but also for stitching. The camera shows the bird making a neat hole in a grass stem with her beak, then pushing the spider's filament through the hole, pulling it around and beginning the process again. She's a precise seamstress. The leaves that she pierces remain alive and green and when she's finished you would never notice the nest—several leaves bent at a slightly unusual angle that close together like the fingers of a hand. The opening lines of Christina Georgina Rossetti's poem 'Birthday'—'My heart is like a singing bird/

Whose nest is in a water'd shoot'—perhaps best images the nest's astonishing beauty.

Another aspect of the TV series is that it reveals how, in nature, many birds have no fear of humans. But they're not all like the skua that attacked Andy Rouse. In one scene, set on the Falkland Islands, Sir David sits demurely on a rock, knees and hands tucked together, next to an albatross nest. While the great birds go about caring for their chick and chatting affectionately to one another, Sir David quietly explains the massive distances they must fly each day to find food for themselves and their young, hundreds of kilometres across the ocean. Sir David has a way with animals, an intuitive, intelligent respect. His admiration for the albatross is unmistakable. He must also be tremendously hardy: he was seventy-two when *The Life of Birds* was made.

Outside of my fantasies, Sir David would probably find me a burden. I have a small store of reckless courage but my energy is nervous and unpredictable. Like many writers, I sleep badly: my mind always outlasts my body. My fine Irish skin burns easily, I tend to droop in the heat and invisible insects are attracted to me, their bites causing rashes and suppurating sores. I also have an unreliable stomach which can take offence at the slightest change in diet. While others are tucking into exotic delicacies, I'll be sipping bottled water and picking my way through the blandest dish (though once in Mexico, for a dare, I did eat ants, served chilled in a vinaigrette, and suffered no ill effects). In short, I need protection from the elements.

In the mid-1980s, Stephen found Cartwright Cottage, perched at the edge of Apollo Bay on Cartwright Street with a grand view over the water, and it became our holiday house which we rented, on and off, for a decade. It takes years to get to know a place, to read its light and weather, its creatures and their habits. I've lived in my part of Elwood for twelve years and if the birds don't teach me something new each day, at least they pique my curiosity. Nature is a jigsaw puzzle and your own section needs to be learned, taken apart, put back together, piece by piece, until you understand how everything fits.

In the city, it's tricky to find a language in which to discuss nature, to share and communicate observations. It seems self-conscious and even corny to exclaim, 'Look, the mudlark's nest!' Perhaps we secretly store our observations, waiting for the right moment to introduce them into conversation. When I discussed the idea for this book with Jane, my publisher, I nervously wondered how she would respond. Did it sound crazy? We were having a drink in an upmarket bar in Sydney. I rattled on for a few moments and then Jane looked at me oddly and said, 'I think birds are amazing, too.' Jane has been my publisher for over a decade and it didn't seem much was excluded from our friendship—in the mix are friends and families, disappointments and dislikes, plus whatever drama is happening with whatever book I'm writing. But we'd never talked about nature, and our feelings for it. With relief, now, I realised I didn't have to explain anything.

Holidays are ideal for nature study. There's no business to be done, only distractions to be had. Stephen and I took our holidays at a leisurely pace. In the morning we wandered down to the town and planned our day over coffee and the newspapers. Apollo Bay has an unpredictable climate due to its proximity to the Otways. One minute it can be sunny; the next, clouds roll down from the mountains, bringing sleet and freezing winds. Sometimes we were imprisoned at Cartwright Cottage all day, waiting for the weather to clear. After succumbing to cabin fever one rainswept afternoon, we decided to take as our role models the Brontë sisters, Charlotte, Emily and Anne, who went tramping over the Yorkshire moors however inclement the weather, with the added encumbrance of their long skirts and cloaks. So we rugged up and sallied forth into the rain—not too bad if you don't head into the wind—and laughed at ourselves so much we nearly fell over in the sand. Years later, Stephen and I recall the Brontë sisters and we still discuss birds.

3
Early birds and bird brains

I HAVE A FONDNESS FOR raptors. Their deadly speed and equally deadly intent make them the purest, swiftest predators of the bird world. The name comes from the Latin *rapere*, which means to seize, to carry off by force or to plunder. They are beautiful outlaws. Ambitious, too. One afternoon in Elwood I pulled over my car to watch a hubbub in the air. A tawny-coloured goshawk had a turtle dove in its talons and was attempting to make off with it while the entire neighbour-hood—magpies, mudlarks and mynas—mobbed the goshawk in a frenzied chorus. They had united not, I believe, to save the turtle dove but to expel an interloper. The goshawk struggled to hold the dove, which was nearly as large as itself, until, accepting defeat, it let go. The dove hit the ground and scuttled under a car. Triumphantly, the other birds chased the goshawk into the sky.

Once I passed beneath a black-shouldered kite as it sat atop a light pole at St Kilda Beach. I looked up at it and it looked fixedly down at me with its ruby-red eyes, giving me the unnerving feeling I was being assessed as a potential meal. (I do apologise, by the way, for the number of personal pronouns in this book. It's partly because I'm no authority and have to rely on my own observations, and partly because I couldn't figure out how else to write it, which probably amounts to the same thing. Anyway, please bear with me.)

One of the most suspenseful scenes in Steven Spielberg's *Jurassic Park* occurs when sister and brother Lex and Tim are hunted by two stealthy Velociraptors in an empty restaurant kitchen. The children's attempts to elude and then outrun the creatures make for nail-biting cinema, especially when the camera gives a close-up of the Velociraptors' eyes: cunning, observant and coolly murderous. In fact, the Velociraptors were not the big clever lizards that Spielberg presents. Nor were they birds but, believed to be predators, they were labelled raptor. The raptors—who existed about 70 million years ago— were around the size of a turkey, covered with feathers and sporting feathered wings. The conceit of the film, and Michael Crichton's novel on which it was based, is that fossilised DNA can be resequenced and cloned: the past can be brought back to life.

The prehistoric bird Archaeopteryx (meaning 'ancient wing') is 150 million years old. In *The Life of Birds*, David Attenborough takes us to the limestone quarry in the Bavarian region of southern Germany where Archaeopteryx was unearthed in 1877. The quarry manager sold the fossil to Ernst Häberlein, an amateur collector, for a pittance. After a bidding war, orchestrated by Häberlein, Archaeopteryx was sold to the Humboldt Museum of Natural History in Berlin where it resides today.

Fittingly, art is behind the discovery of this, the first bird. The prints that John and Elizabeth Gould made for their high-quality illustrations required limestone—the perfect medium for detailed lithographic printing. Solnhofen, where Archaeopteryx was found, has been quarried for paving stones since Roman times. But, as anthropologist Pat Shipman points out, it was only when lithography became popular in the nineteenth century that the fine-grained stones were rendered valuable rather than just useful. Solnhofen limestone is so smooth that it will take the sharpest lines, conveying the subtlest textures that can be created by the artist's hand. As a result, a painstaking process of hand-quarrying began (and continues today) that led directly to the discovery of Archaeopteryx and many other fine fossils. Each slab of

Solnhofen limestone is chiselled out by hand, split, inspected for flaws, sorted, and then often trimmed further to the exact dimensions required for the printing process. From start to finish, sometimes as many as a dozen skilled quarrymen examine each surface of each slab with care; as a result, even if they are not intentionally sought fossils are not missed as Pat Shipman notes. 'Only the coincidence of the artist and of Archaeopteryx accounts for this fact.'[1] More mechanical quarrying—the rule elsewhere—would have certainly destroyed the fossil.

Archaeopteryx is dazzling. Caught in stone, the skeleton appears to be dancing in graceful abandon on its long, elegant legs. With its head thrown back, its wings swirl like diaphanous veils from its raised arms. Pat Shipman memorably describes it as a 'two-dimensional sculpture of a fabulous chimera, half-bird, half-reptile' showing 'ligaments, tendons, skin and feathers pressed almost flat between the rocks of the ages'.[2]

Archaeopteryx is such an important find because it marks the evolutionary transition between reptiles and birds: it shows feathers attached to the body. About the size of a magpie, it has a reptilian head with bony jaws and teeth but it walked and perched like a bird, perhaps even glided. Archaeopteryx wasn't the first creature that flew: that honour belongs to the insects. Pterosaurs (winged lizards) coexisted with Archaeopteryx for millions of years—some lived alongside Archaeopteryx in the

Solnhofen lagoon—but the great sails of the pterosaurs' wings were made of skin and if they hit the water as they hunted for fish, they could drown. Nor could the pterosaurs compete with the ability of Archaeopteryx to feed in the restricted terrain of the forest, one of the many factors that contributed to the pterosaurs' demise. With its mix of old, reptilian features and new, birdlike assets Archaeopteryx was destined to (briefly) become a winner in the struggle for survival. Darwin had the good fortune to be able to comment on Archaeopteryx, 'this strange bird', in the fourth edition of *On the Origin of Species*. Subsequently, Archaeopteryx became a key piece of evidence in the debate over evolution.

There are two hypotheses about the ancestry of the first bird. Archaeopteryx was descended either from the dinosaurs, which is known as the 'ground up' hypothesis, or from a tree-dwelling glider, known as the 'trees down' hypothesis. Both theories have been hotly contested. But a remarkable discovery in China in 1996 has convinced many of the 'ground up' argument. In the remote hills of Liaoning province, north-east of Beijing, fossils of small feathered dinosaurs have been found that are around 124 million years old. While Archaeopteryx is older and did not descend from the feathered dinosaurs, this shows that some species of dinosaurs were developing avian characteristics. Next time you see an aggressive bird like a myna hopping about the streets, remember—once were dinosaurs.

We also know that dinosaurs made nests. In 2006, had you been cashed up you could have purchased a 65-million-year-old dinosaur nest in mint condition from an auction house in Los Angeles. It would have set you back US$420,000. The nest, unearthed in Guangdong province in southern China, had been restored to museum quality by its owner, and embryonic remains were revealed in most of the twenty-two eggs. Some eggs were so well preserved that the curled-up embryos were visible inside. The female dinosaur made a circular depression in moist earth where she deposited the eggs, usually in a circle around the edge. In some cases, it is thought the parent settled herself on top to keep them warm and brooded the young until they hatched. In others, she covered the eggs with vegetation or allowed natural forces like sun or the mud in which the eggs were buried to create the right temperature for incubation. Many spectacular dinosaur nesting sites have been discovered from Mongolia to Argentina. In some cases, entire nesting colonies have been preserved because they were caught in natural disasters like sandstorms, floods or volcanic eruptions.

The Oviraptor, discovered in Mongolia in the 1920s, was mistakenly given the name of 'egg thief' because that's what she seemed to be doing—stealing eggs from a nest. Recently, it's been considered that the skeleton, found poised above the nest, could have been a brooding parent protecting her own eggs rather than trying to eat them. Around the same size as a Velociraptor, she had a beak that made her look like a big perky parrot and she may have had feathers. Maiasaura had better luck in the naming stakes. Discovered in northern Montana, she was the subject of a book co-authored by Jack Horner, the palaeontologist adviser for the *Jurassic Park* movies. Poetically named for the Greek goddess Maia, the mother of Hermes, *Maiasaura* roughly means 'good mother lizard'. She was so named because she supplied the first proof that giant dinosaurs raised and fed their young.[3] Eighty million years ago, Maiasaura lived in flocks and bred in nesting colonies packed closely together like those of modern seabirds such as silver gulls or albatrosses.

Horner discovered that the Maiasaura females gathered in birdlike flocks before building their nests, which were spaced seven metres apart. First the Maiasaurs made mounds almost two metres wide which they hollowed out for the eggs. The females then arranged vegetation, covering the nest and keeping the eggs warm until they hatched. The babies had to stay in the nest for at least a month until they were large enough to fend for themselves, and both parents must have stayed nearby to protect them from predators.

I asked Professor Patricia Vickers-Rich for her opinion about Horner's research. Pat trained at San Francisco's Berkeley University before joining Monash University where she founded the Monash Science Centre and where she has a chair of palaeontology. Pat is a warm, brisk, good-humoured woman with a mop of silvery-gold hair and clear blue eyes. Her husband, Dr Thomas Rich, is a senior curator at the Melbourne Museum. They're a formidable team. In 2000, *National Geographic* awarded them the Committee for Research and Exploration Chairman's Award in recognition of 'their tireless and virtually superhuman efforts to gather and interpret fossils of great significance'.[4]

Since the 1980s, Pat and Tom have been working on a site called Dinosaur Dreaming near Inverloch on the Victorian coast. Teams of volunteers, under the direction of Leslie Kool, make annual digs which have yielded fertile results. There's been the discovery of the small theropod *Leaellynasaura*, which Pat and Tom named after their daughter, Leaellyn, and the mysterious ornithomimid *Timimus*, named for their son. When Pat and Tom ran out of children to name their dinosaurs after, they turned to the national airline and called a two-legged, plant-eating dinosaur *Qantassaurus*.

Pat was the first person with whom I discussed this book. I thought if people were going to consider me crazy for saying that birds are artists, I might as well start at the top. Pat and I met over coffee on campus and I babbled, a fault of mine when I'm nervous, especially in the presence of an august individual. Pat gently corrected my ignorance—all sorts of creatures make nests and birds were *not* the first—plus she wasn't comfortable with the whole notion of 'firsts' anyway. When I outlined the idea for the book, she was disarmingly encouraging. I've found that imaginative folk, in whatever academic discipline or walk of life you meet them, have few boundaries when it comes to unusual ideas. Such adventurously-minded people make great teachers and are heartening to be around. When I asked Pat if I was taking up too much of her time with my dumb questions, she laughed, 'No, you're cute!' Pat and Tom have not found dinosaur nests at their site. She supports Horner's conclusions but points out that questions remain: did feathered dinosaurs exist in the Mesozoic era? Did theropods make nests?

In the late 1990s, palaeontologists Luis Chiappe and Lowell Dingus discovered a vast dinosaur hatchery in the rocky south Argentine desert. They'd gone searching for fossilised birds but instead stumbled upon a nursery that stretched for kilometres. There were so many eggs, it was difficult to take a step without breaking one. Around 90 million years ago, hundreds if not thousands of giant sauropod dinosaurs had gathered to build nests in a fertile plain cut with shallow streams. Those dinosaurs did not incubate the nest—they let the sun do that, rather like modern alligators. At birth, the baby sauropod dinosaur was around 40 centimetres in length, and grew to a whopping 30 metres long.

Among modern birds, the brush turkey, another large megapode bird, also makes a mound of twigs, leaf litter and soil, in this case a hatchery with a precisely controlled temperature. Their name literally means large foot (Greek: *mega* = large, *poda* = foot) and refers to the heavy legs and feet typical of these flightless birds. The brush turkey's destruction of the bowerbird's nest was mentioned in the first chapter; as the male turkey takes five months to make its own nest, an extraordinarily long period of time for avian construction, it made me wonder, watching him create havoc in the bowerbird's boudoir, whether some element of competition was involved. With his powerful legs, the brush turkey flicks his nest into shape, periodically flattening and compacting it, until he has built a mound around four metres in diameter and over one metre high. Take that, satin bowerbird! In the warm damp forest, the nest rapidly ferments; while the temperature is initially much higher than necessary for incubation, it gradually falls until it is thirty-three degrees Celsius. That's no accident either as the brush turkey, who has a heat sensor inside his upper bill, digs test holes to check the heat. If it's too hot, he removes material to allow heat to escape and if it's too cool, he heaps more onto the mound.

By domesticating some animals, we have formed great alliances. The horse changed human history. Wolves became dogs and thus our best friends. Cats, with their vanity and self-possession, seem to have chosen us. Birds, however, unless we cage them, are not usually interested in being tamed. Maybe the cockatoo, with its intelligence and its wry sense of humour, takes pleasure in being our companion, perched in a living room and mimicking our voices after its wings have been clipped; pigeons, docile and amiable, have been trained for centuries. Like many Australian children, I grew up with caged budgerigars as pets. Poor Bluey—as he or she was inevitably named—never lasted very long. Either we fed him too much or too little or the cat harassed him to death. It's a practice I now find odious: birds are not *meant* to be kept in cages. But many species of birds prefer to leave a habitat than to try to adapt to our ways. Adaptation through natural selection has not made birds keen to associate with us or to become our pets.

Ravens are something of an exception, as Charles Dickens knew. In *Barnaby Rudge*, the eponymous protagonist has a pet raven called Grip that he carries in a basket on his back. Dickens confessed that Grip was 'a compound of two great originals, of whom I was, at different times, the proud possessor'. Dickens' first raven slept in the stable, preferably on horseback, and so terrified Dickens' dog that the bird could, 'by the mere superiority of his genius', walk off unmolested with the dog's dinner, literally swiped from beneath the dog's nose. After that raven's accidental death, Dickens was inconsolable until a friend found in a pub in Yorkshire another tame raven, 'older and more gifted', that he bought for Dickens. After raven number two had dug up all the cheese and coins that his predecessor had buried in the garden—'a work of immense labour and research, to which he devoted all the energies of his mind'—the bird then 'applied himself to the acquisition of [coach-driver's] language, in which he soon became such an adept, that he would perch outside my window and drive imaginary horses with great skill, all day.'[5]

The intelligence of crows is well documented and, like the satin bowerbird, they have been the subject of scientific research. Distinguishing between 'raven' and 'crow' is rather confusing. Crows account for the entire family of birds known as corvids, which includes the raven species, and while that means all ravens are crows, crows can be ravens, jays or rooks. In Australia, we call Australian ravens 'crows' and the only major difference between them and their Northern Hemisphere relatives is their white eyes. Crows evolved in central Asia and then spread through Australia, Europe, Africa and North America. It depends on the poetic leaning of the writer which name they assign the bird. Edgar Allan Poe's 'Raven' is a gothic figure of paranoid hallucination to the melancholic young man whom it visits. By the poem's end, as the young man descends into delusion, the raven proves to be a psychopomp to an underworld of madness. Ted Hughes' post-Holocaustal Crow, from his cycle *From the Life and Songs of the Crow*, is a bleak, amoral, Dionysian man-bird who can outwit both God and death, and who boasts about it.

In myth and folklore, crows have been represented as tricksters and, latterly and more fearfully, as portents of doom and embodiments of destruction and violence. But their intelligence is never in doubt. *The Epic of Gilgamesh*, the Mesopotamian poem which dates from the third millennium BC, is the earliest record of human literature. On his journey to seek eternal life, Gilgamesh meets Utnapishtim, who has survived a terrifying flood which the gods loosed to destroy mankind. To test the waters had receded, Utnapishtim first released a dove, which returned, then a swallow, and finally a raven, which provided the necessary proof. 'She saw that the waters had retreated, she ate, she flew around, she cawed and she did not come back.'[6]

To Native American people on the Pacific Northwest Coast the raven is a powerful creator figure, whose myth, similar to a tale about a raven in Ovid's *Metamorphoses*, explains how the bird, once white, became black. In the Haida people's version of the story, Raven seeks to save humanity by stealing the sun, the moon and the stars, as well as a firebrand, from

Grey Eagle, who hated humans and kept the valuable items to himself. After hanging the sun in the sky and then fastening the moon there after the sun had set, Raven flew across the world with the firebrand, the smoke causing his feathers to turn black. In Roman mythology, the raven's fate is a judgement on its chattering indiscretion. Once of a 'silvery hue, with such snowy feathers that it could rival any spotless dove', the bird was turned black as a punishment by Apollo after it informed him that his lover Coronis had been unfaithful.[7] (Coronis fared much worse: Apollo killed her with an arrow.) In both tales, the birds are messengers and in the latter, one that's too smart for its own good. Interestingly, before the raven is changed to sable by Apollo, a crow, who was herself human before being transformed into a bird, warns the raven of the danger of telling tales, even if it's done with the best of intentions. The raven ignores her advice.

The reputation of crows as evil angels is historically well founded, based on the birds' predilection for carrion. Soldiers going into battle knew that if they died their bodies could be scavenged by crows. During the fourteenth century, the population of Europe was decimated by the bubonic plague, history's worst pandemic, which took around 100 million lives. It was not a pretty sight. Stinking corpses riddled with sores that had oozed black pus were dragged from their houses, or from the streets where they fell, and flung on the carts destined for the hastily dug mass graves. The crows were there, waiting for the dead. Perhaps this is why a flock of crows is known as a 'murder', while the collective noun for ravens is an 'unkindness' or a 'storytelling'. The English seem to have quelled their fear of ravens, and several magnificent examples, standing at around a metre high, provide a tourist attraction at the Tower of London. (The tale that England will fall without their presence, ascribed to Charles II, is perhaps due to their reputation as messengers, nosey, noisy, alert reporters.) Attended by their personal Ravenmaster who feeds them raw meat and biscuits soaked in blood, the birds spend each night in a raven hotel. In such luxurious surroundings, the birds can live up to forty years. However, not all the ravens make the grade. In 1986, Raven George was dismissed for 'conduct unsatisfactory' and sent to the Welsh Mountain Zoo.[8] He'd been caught demolishing television aerials.

Over the centuries, as humans needed to hunt less, our relationship with crows changed, a factor which may account for their demonisation. To the Inuit, ravens were once part of their hunting strategy, the birds often alerting them to the presence of prey such as caribou or polar bears. The Inuit believed that if they invoked the ravens with a secret name imparted by a shaman, the bird would assist them. The hunters rewarded the birds by leaving choice morsels for them to eat. Odin, ruler of the Norse gods, was also known as the Raven god. He kept a bird on each shoulder, named Hugin (thought), and Munin (memory). Every morning Odin sent them far and wide: they ranged across the inhabited world, questioning the living and the dead, returning at evening to bring their master the news of the world, like an ancient version of Wikileaks. They also accompanied Odin into battle. For the Vikings, ravens were omens for a successful raid. In his book *Mind of the Raven*, Bernd Heinrich, a biologist who can only be described as a raven-obsessive, recounts an Eskimo tale. A hunter who wants to settle near some seal breathing holes he has found in the ice is told by a raven precisely where to camp. The hunter foolishly heeds the raven and camps where directed. In the night he is killed by a boulder falling from the mountain above. The raven then flies down and pecks out the hunter's eyes, saying, 'I don't know why all these hunters believe my silly stories.'[9]

There's plenty of anecdotal evidence for the cleverness of crows. In 1999, Ann and Wallace Collito from North Attleboro, Massachusetts, found an abandoned black and white kitten wandering in their garden. The following day they were astonished when the kitten trotted into the yard accompanied by a crow. As the cat relaxed on the lawn, the crow hunted for worms and, very carefully, fed them to her. When the Collitos told their disbelieving vet of what they'd seen, he encouraged them to make a video; the result is on

YouTube. The crow, perhaps itself an orphan, has assumed the role of parent, feeding and caring for the kitten. As the pair cross the road, the crow becomes anxious that the kitten is straggling and gives her a peck to make her move faster. The crow and the kitten roll in the grass, teasing one another and playing hilarious games of hide and seek. When Ann Collito began feeding the kitten meat, the crow ate too, but only after it had made sure that the kitten had eaten her fill.

Groundbreaking new research offers insights into crows' canniness. Nicky Clayton is Professor of Comparative Cognition in the Department of Experimental Psychology at Cambridge University and a fellow of the Royal Society, the United Kingdom's oldest and most prestigious society for science. Her research on the behaviour of jays, a crow relative, has led her to believe that they have complex cognitive abilities such as episodic memory—the recall of an actual moment in time rather than simply the ability to learn a skill or a fact. Episodic memory uses the same structures in the human brain's hippocampus as does imagination. It demonstrates the capacity for mental time travel, the ability to recall past events or envision new ones. Clayton's experiments, reports Charles Wohlforth, raise for the first time the possibility that jays can mentally time travel too. 'We thought these abilities were uniquely human. The fact that jays have them says no,' Clayton comments.[10]

Clayton has focused on the jays' ability to hide and then find food, a technique called 'caching'. Collaborating with Tony Dickinson, a comparative psychologist at Cambridge, Clayton showed in 1998 that the cognitive capacities of the scrub jays she studied included the ability to negotiate the passage of time. She found that the birds would return to caches when the food they had hidden was about to spoil. The jays also adjusted their retrieval pattern when presented with new information about how quickly a certain food goes bad, abandoning those caches whose contents had passed their use-by dates.[11]

Together with her husband Dr Nathan Emery, a research fellow at Cambridge, Clayton has investigated the latent intelligence of corvids by testing rooks, which do not use tools in the wild, with complex tasks requiring tools. With each step in Emery and Clayton's laboratory experiments, the challenges got harder and more complicated, and the rooks solved every one. In an experiment inspired by Aesop's fables, the rooks were presented with a worm floating out of reach in a large tube of water. The birds put rocks in the tube to raise the water level to capture the worm. They even manufactured tools, bending a wire to make a hook to pull a bucket holding food out of the tube. The tool worked only with a bend of precise curvature, around a hundred degrees. Emery comments, 'We wouldn't have expected that at all . . . It is an example of insight. It's coming up with a novel solution, to innovate.'[12] Indeed, Clayton and Emery have argued that the intelligence of corvids is on a par with that of non-human apes, and the pair refer to them as 'feathered apes'.[13]

Clayton's connection with birds goes beyond the laboratory. She's a scientist by day and a tango dancer by night. In 2009, her twin passions for birds and dance combined when she was invited by London's Rambert Dance Company to collaborate with artistic director Mark Baldwin on the choreography of a new work. She taught the dancers 'tango moves inspired by our feathered friends'.[14] The result was a dance performance, *The Comedy of Change*, that celebrated Darwin's bicentenary.[15] Birds, Clayton observes, spend a lot of time dancing. The male blue manakin of Argentina, fittingly the home of the tango, are reported to spend about 90 per cent of their time dancing, with moves that take them around eight years to perfect and that are taught by an older male. The dancing is not only concerned with natural selection but sexual selection as well. In the branches, the males perform elaborate dancing duels observed by an audience of critical females—'only the top-notch dancers get to mate'.[16]

If corvids are so clever, what kind of nests do they make? At his home in Vermont, Bernd Heinrich had the good fortune to watch two of his tamed ravens build a nest and breed. Fuzz and Houdi were crazy about each other, preening one another constantly and spending all their time together. (Preening has a practical purpose—the bird's sharp beak cleans the parasites from its mate's feathers—and it's also an intimate bonding ritual, similar to the grooming that apes perform on one another. For humans, it would be the next best thing to holding hands and smooching, signifying pleasure in and possession of one's partner.) In Heinrich's large aviary, Houdi, the female, selected a site inside a shed where she deposited several twigs while Fuzz watched attentively. Over the following weeks, Fuzz alone did the work of carrying the sticks and arranging them, rather casually, in a basket-like shape. There was as much play as work involved and Heinrich wondered whether the two were up to the serious business of making a nest and starting a family. What was missing? During winter in the wild, ravens insulate their deep nests with the soft warmth of fur. To help the couple along, Heinrich placed in the aviary an old sheepskin. Both birds examined the material intently. Houdi shredded some of the wool before depositing it in the nest while Fuzz grabbed sticks and carried them to the nest. The sheepskin triggered a burst of activity and the birds began building the nest with a will and lining it with the wool. Heinrich also supplied the birds with dead grass—which Houdi carried to the nest in one large load—and a stick of wood from an ash tree, which she stripped of bark before arranging it in the nest. The final result was impressive, more than half a metre high, with a nest cup measuring fifteen centimetres. A few weeks later, Houdi lay five pear-shaped, sea-coloured eggs; Fuzz fed her while she brooded. When the nestlings hatched, both parents catered for them by tearing meat from animal carcasses supplied by Heinrich, and fed themselves only once the babies were replete.

Though wild ravens choose a crag or a tree, crows, as urban dwellers, are pragmatists and can nest on powerlines, on radar towers, on buildings above busy streets, under highway overpasses and in abandoned buildings. Crows' nests are sometimes described as untidy, perhaps due to the preponderance of twigs protruding at all angles, but, as Lyanda Lynn Haupt points out, up close the effect is more intricate, purposeful and mandala-like than it appears from below. She also observed that, where she was able to distinguish male from female, the female manages most of the fine-tuning in the arrangement of nest sticks. The female accomplishes this secretly after the male, satisfied with the placement, has flown off to gather more. She watches him leave, then moves his most recent additions to suit her own taste. Haupt reasons, 'We females normally have to brood the young . . . It makes sense that we would be fussier about what sticks were poking us where.'[17] After arranging the nest sticks in the fork of a tree, Haupt's crow neighbours then lined their nests with bark, moss, pieces of string or yarn, shreds of paper and, occasionally, fur from roadkill. Perhaps the exterior is armoured like a bulwark against predators—raptors such as eagles and owls are especially fond of corvids—and the deep, safe, warm pocket assures the nestlings the best chance of survival.

I'm thankful to Haupt for her records because crows are secretive about their nest building and I've had little luck in observing them. Walking back to my car from busy South Melbourne Market one Sunday morning, I observed a crow stripping a large twig from a tree branch above my head. I put down my bags and gazed upwards. As soon as the crow saw that I was watching, it stopped its work and cawed loudly for its mate. The mate duly arrived and the two had a conference—probably along the lines of, 'Bloody human! Why doesn't she take her shopping and get lost?' Then they flew to the cornice of a nearby building and waited until I picked up my bags and walked away.

4
Migrants and writers

THE NEIGHBOURS ARE DRIVING ME crazy. In the first chapter I mentioned the mynas which live in the air vent in my study and I waxed lyrical about their dulcet tones in the evening. In mid-spring they gave birth to a gaggle of babies that squeak constantly, even more loudly when Mum and Dad approach the nest with food, which occurs innumerable times a day. Awake before me, the children are shrieking at seven am when I totter into the study, half-asleep, to check the overnight emails. As the day wears on, I'm driven from the study by the chirruping. As I write, it's nightfall and a degree of calm has settled on the nest. No more feeding forays for the exhausted parents, though the kids continue to pester them. Mum and Dad are hyped, protective, and when I enter the backyard, they swoop down to monitor my movements. 'I get it, okay?' I snap. 'You're rearing the kids. *But can you keep the noise down?*' We glare at one another from opposite sides of the yard. Thankfully, most chicks grow fast, so within another week they'll have fledged and taken to the skies.

The nesting of birds is a potent symbol of hope and renewal, especially in the case of the swallow, which inspired the cautious proverb, 'One swallow doesn't make a summer.' This reflects the longing for summer during the bitter winters of the Northern Hemisphere, the disappointment when a lone arrival in the spring did not presage a flock or a change in the weather. Don't get your hopes up!

Virginia Woolf, who had a country house on the Sussex Downs, experienced a rapturous, sensual delight in the natural world that she recorded in her fiction, essays, letters and diaries. She was also a knowledgeable birdwatcher, mining their behaviour for her work. She observed the rooks 'beating up against the wind', which made her say to herself instinctively, 'Whats [*sic*] the phrase for that?' Woolf sought to capture in words the vivid roughness of the air currents and the tremor of the rooks 'as if the air were full of ridges & ripples'. It seemed the rooks took pleasure in the movement, rubbing and bracing against the air currents 'like swimmers in rough water'.[1] Virginia's enthusiasm for Sussex drew her friends there, making it the Bloomsbury country residence.

Woolf's element was air—she was cerebral, quick-witted, flirtatious, gossipy and mischievous. Her husband Leonard commented how Virginia swooped like a bird between reality and romance 'which join inextricably to join her'. He wrote poems describing her 'as a clean, ethereal creature, a spirit at one with the wind and the wide sky over the Downs'.[2] The popular image of Virginia—cooped up in a room having yet another nervous breakdown—is at odds with her physical stamina: she was hardy, fit, an enthusiastic walker and cyclist and, as a young woman, a demon bowler.

Woolf's final work, *Between the Acts*, which is set in 'the heart of the country', takes place on a single summer's day in the garden of a grand manor where the local people perform their annual pageant, scenes from the history of England.[3] There's no plot, only the day's progress and the scenes from the pageant, interwoven with conversations and reflections by the characters. Nature is a radiant companion to the action as Woolf compresses it into metaphors that illuminate her human characters. A man leaning 'silent, sardonic' against a door is like 'a withered willow'; a talkative woman suddenly becomes 'solemn as an owl'.[4] Birds are everywhere—'chuckling over the substance and succulence of the day' or 'attacking the dawn like so many choir boys an iced cake'.[5] A line of trees is 'an open-air cathedral', where the darting swallows seemed to dance, 'only not to music but to the unheard rhythm of their wild hearts'.[6] Nature is paradise lost, a transcendent realm of beauty and goodness that Woolf's alienated characters, who brood over the past, over their disappointments and misunderstandings, are unable to reach. Even when the characters are granted flashes of insight and sympathy, they are often unable to express them, underscoring their tragic separateness from one another. Unlike the joyfully industrious birds who revel in their sense of community, the humans are doomed to separateness.

Lucy Swithin is 'an old lady with a high nose, thin cheeks, a ring on her finger and the usual trappings of a rather shabby but gallant old age, which included in her case a cross gleaming gold on her breast'.[7] Attuned to birds in general and the swallows in particular, Mrs Swithin earns the scorn of a fellow guest at the pageant when she comments on the swallows building their nests in the barn. 'They come every year,' Lucy Swithin tells Mrs Manresa, who 'smiled benevolently, humouring the old lady's whimsy. It was unlikely, she thought, that the birds were the same.'[8] But Lucy Swithin was right, as Woolf knew: swallows *do* return to their former nesting places. The passage also contrasts the childlike enthusiasm of Lucy, the imaginative birdwatcher, with the sophisticated Mrs Manresa who is ignorant of nature. Nor does Woolf let Mrs Manresa get away with it. When Mrs Manresa excuses herself—'I'm dying for my tea!'—Lucy continues, '"They come every year", ignoring the fact that she spoke to empty air . . . Across Africa, across France they had come to nest there. Year after year they came. Before there was a channel, when the earth was a riot of rhododendrons, and humming birds quivered at the mouths of scarlet trumpets . . . they had come.'[9]

The migration of birds has been taking place since the first ice age, seventy thousand years ago, and probably long before that. Ornithologist Guilhem Lesaffre estimates that five billion European birds of around two hundred species leave to winter in Africa each year. But this number represents only about a tenth of the world's total population of migrating birds.[10] The reasons for migrating—to escape the privations of winter and to find new feeding grounds—are clear, certainly in the case of swallows, which eat only insects. Barn swallows, Virginia's birds, have a global distribution with a population of around 190 million. They're relatives of the swallows that I've watched nest in the corridor near the cafeteria at Monash University. But as Australian winters are not harsh, this species—the welcome swallow—migrates only a few hundred kilometres north. Virginia's swallows set off on much more arduous journeys.

Swallows are about the size of your hand and weigh less than thirty grams. They have iridescent blue feathers, chestnut-coloured faces and two elegant tail feathers that stream behind them like ribbons. They are graceful flyers with superb skills—swooping, darting and gliding in wayward arcs. Departing England in October, they travel in huge flocks through western France, across the Pyrenees, and then to eastern Spain before crossing into Morocco. Some avoid the Sahara by tracking along the coast of western Africa; others fly straight over the desert to reach southern Africa. In Aristotle's *History of Animals*, written in 350 BC, he first classified barn swallows as migratory though he believed they hibernated, a fallacy that was repeated for centuries. Their route was confirmed as recently as 1912, when an amateur naturalist James Masefield ringed a swallow at a nest in Staffordshire and the bird was later found in Natal. For centuries, humans couldn't understand where the birds went. Was this because we didn't believe birds could undertake such perilous and complex navigations? Because our imagination did not allow us to take flight?

Looking at an atlas and tracing the swallows' journey is a daunting experience, especially following the birds' path once they have reached Morocco: the toughest part is still ahead, across the waterless wastes of the Sahara—a quicker though more dangerous route than skirting the coast—and on through Algeria, Niger, Chad, Cameroon, Democratic Republic of Congo, Zambia and Zimbabwe to finally reach, in the case of the Staffordshire swallow, the province of Natal. That journey alone is more than seven thousand kilometres.

Add the flight from England to Morocco and it's nearly ten thousand kilometres. The birds band together for protection and travel only by day. Many die from starvation and exhaustion or in storms. Migrating swallows can cover about three hundred kilometres a day at speeds of around thirty kilometres per hour.[11] There's no mad rush and the journey is spread over a month.

The birds have evolved a navigational system that uses sunlight. They also memorise topography and recognise landmarks such as coastlines, rivers, wetlands and mountain ranges. They watch for the patterns of islands and of waves. They also have an inbuilt compass which helps them to sense the earth's magnetic field, so they can determine absolute north, and to judge the direction of light—and thus the sun's position—even when the day is overcast. Their acute hearing means they perceive infrasound (sounds lower in frequency than twenty Hertz), which allows them to navigate using the noise of waves from a distant sea, the wind from a mountain range or the soft contact calls of birds nearby.[12] But not all their skills have been uncovered by science. No one knows, for example, exactly how they navigate the Sahara.

I envy the swallows their vision of the landscape. Once I flew from Johannesburg to Nairobi, a distance of nearly three thousand kilometres over the majestic body of Africa, with the glittering Indian Ocean to the right. When the snow-covered slopes of Mount Kilimanjaro came into view, it meant we were approaching the border of Tanzania and Kenya. The plateau of southern Kenya looks as calm, green and welcoming as an English park. The plane cruises at high altitudes while the swallows fly low to take advantage of the air currents and to facilitate an easy descent for food, water and rest. What they see we have never seen, the Africa of the swallows.

Not only are the birds faithful to their final destinations, returning to the same place each year, but they also return to favourite stopovers. They swoop down on Boje-Enyi, a small village in south-east Nigeria which lies on the border with Cameroon. In 1995, a detailed study was coordinated by the World Wildlife Fund for Nature and Pro-Natura International, an aid agency. Dr John Ash, an ornithologist involved in the study, recalls the birds' spectacular arrival. 'What are seen initially as almost invisible black spots in the evening sky above Boje-Enyi's grassy hill slopes, gradually increase in number until the horizon is black with hundreds of thousands of birds spiralling down into the grass to sleep.'[13]

Not only did Dr Ash and his team ring three thousand swallows, they also interviewed the swallow hunters. Between December and May, the villagers catch and eat the birds, which supply their diets with much-needed protein. The village conducts its own sustainability program: only the children are allowed to trap the birds, and only when the birds have settled in large numbers. Hunting is restricted to bright moon nights, which means that most nights there is no hunting. At the end of April, Dr Ash's survey showed no significant reduction in swallow numbers.

As autumn wanes in the Southern Hemisphere, the swallows, plump and rested, decide, by mutual consent, to return to Europe. They don't set out all at once but in waves, as they arrived. Why not stay? Natal's winter isn't freezing like that of Sussex. What evolutionary drive determines the resumption of such a dangerous journey? Nearly half of the adults and most of their offspring will die en route. It's also a much quicker passage on the way back: the holidays are over and time is of the essence.

The swallows' relationship with humans has been very successful and they are not an endangered species. By evolving their nest-building to incorporate our architecture, the birds have come to rely on human structures to build their own. They have taken advantage of human settlement, which—unlike the situation for so many birds—has enhanced rather than destroyed their habitat. They also require a plentiful supply of shallow water for their chief building material: mud. Without the overhanging protection of a building, a mud nest would dissolve in the rain. The swallows need us and use us. The breeding cycle is about to begin. It's one of the reasons they hurry back to England—to build, breed and eat their fill in a never-ending cycle of spring and summer.

The males arrive at their destination first, usually their former home, and select a nest site which they loudly display to the females. The females choose a partner via sexual selection—the ones with the longest tail feathers usually win. In this case, size does count; the male with longer tail feathers is a genetically stronger individual who will live longer and has a better immune system to combat disease, giving the offspring enhanced vitality. The nest is a product of teamwork, both partners collecting tiny mud pellets in their beaks and mixing them with long grasses to form a cup shape that they compact against a wall.

As James Gould, professor of ecology and evolutionary biology at Princeton University, and his wife, science writer Carol Grant Gould, observe, the building behaviour itself requires skill and determination. The bird often scrabbles desperately, using its tail not only for balance but as a source of resistance as gravity inexorably pulls it down. Whatever the bird does it must not yield to the temptation of grabbing hold of mud applied only that day, which is still moist and sure to peel off. The swallows typically build in the morning and feed for the rest of the day, leaving their work to harden overnight. By building from the outside in, the swallows crossed 'a dramatic cognitive threshold' in their evolutionary development and passed 'a classic test of intelligence'—the ability to imagine an object or a structure from a new perspective.[14] The nest is then snugly lined with soft, clean feathers. But, rather like the crow, the female swallow is chief architect and decorator. Perhaps she has evolved better taste.

Nature is gendered but not sexist. It might be violent, brutal and unfair but the oppression of females by males has never existed. The laws of nature are not the laws of man. While there's no morality in the animal kingdom and very little compassion, equally there's no sexual discrimination. Whether you are male or female carries no inherent value: it does not necessarily make a creature stronger, swifter, more intelligent or more attractive. In nature, sex does not have to mean destiny.

In *Between the Acts*, Woolf documents her own pleasure at the swallows' return, personifying herself as the endearing but slightly dotty Lucy Swithin. The novel is a palimpsest of voices—those of Lucy and the other characters, plus the swallows. What did the birds' annual migration mean to Woolf? The journey as a metaphor for an individual's life was charted in her first novel, *The Voyage Out*, published in 1915. The sudden death of the protagonist, Rachel Vinrace, suggests that her yearnings, her romantic idealism are inadequate to deal with life's demands. In *Between the Acts*, Woolf's last work, voyaging becomes the province of birds not humans, animals who pragmatically assess the risks of migration and may also die in its completion. But *Between the Acts* does not register such failure. Instead it celebrates the swallows' return and, against all the odds, the triumph of familial bonds and the cherished security of home.

During the Second World War, Virginia and Leonard had settled at their country retreat, Monk's House in the village of Rodmell. London was under attack and their home in Mecklenburgh Square had been bombed. At Monk's House, Virginia wrote in a little weatherboard study which she called the Lodge, situated in the garden under the chestnut tree against the churchyard wall. It gave her sweeping views across the meadows.

The threat of invasion and the extensive bombings were making Virginia increasingly anxious. Sussex, on the flight path of German bombers on their way to London, was targeted. On several occasions, the planes flew directly over Monk's House and bombs shook the windows of her study. Five German raiders flew so low that they brushed the tree by the gate and the swastikas painted on the planes' undercarriage were clearly visible. Suicide was planned in case of a Nazi victory: Adrian Stephen, Virginia's younger brother, a doctor and a psychoanalyst, had given the Woolfs enough morphine to avoid being taken prisoner. During the winter, as Virginia's spirits drooped, she took refuge in nature. 'I worshipped the beauty of the country . . . How England consoles and warms one.'[15] Anorexia, the pinched companion to Virginia's depression, meant she became extremely thin, a condition not helped by food rationing. The severity of the winter also meant she was constantly cold.

In February 1941, Woolf finished revising *Between the Acts*. The distance between the radiant summer she pictured and her current circumstances must have seemed immense, as far away as the Africa of the swallows. She decided it was a worthless book and wrote to her publisher John Lehmann telling him not to publish it as it stood because 'its [*sic*] too silly and trivial'.[16] As Leonard knew, when Virginia completed a book she was most vulnerable to depression. As the darkness in her mind deepened, Virginia wrote in terror to her sister Vanessa Bell: 'I feel that I have gone too far this time to come back again. I am certain now that I am going mad again. It is just as it was the first time, I am always hearing voices . . . I can hardly think clearly any more . . . I have fought against it, but I cant [sic] any longer.'[17]

Late in March, Virginia wrote notes for Vanessa and Leonard that she placed in her study. Then she put on her coat, took her walking stick and hurried out. When I visited Monk's House some years ago, I did her final walk. It's not far—through the gate, past the churchyard and across the water meadows to the river. It was the start of Woolf's favourite

Bower of a great satin bowerbird, Irvinebank, Queensland   (PHOTOGRAPH © TIM LAMAN)

Lesser masked weaver making a nest, southern Africa

Sociable weavers' nest, Kalahari Desert, Namibia

Barn swallows in a nest

Storks' nest, Alsace, France

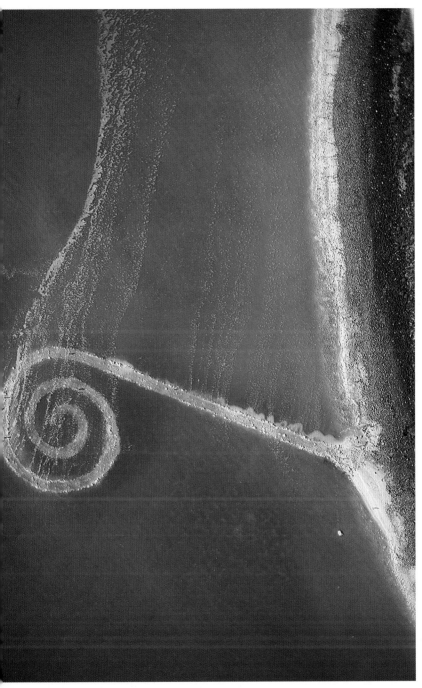

Robert Smithson, *Spiral Jetty* (1970)

Archaeopteryx lithographica

MUSEUM FÜR NATURKUNDE LEIBNIZ-INSTITUT FÜR EVOLUTIONS UND BIODIVERSITÄTSFORSCHUNG
AN DER HUMBOLDT-UNIVERSITÄT, BERLIN

Antarctic skua, Antarctica   (PHOTOGRAPH © ANDY ROUSE/NATUREPL.COM)

Pine siskin's nest (c. 1924)

Striped honeyeater's nest (c. 1969)

Skylark's nest

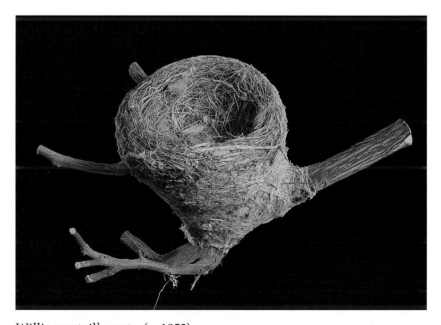

Willie wagtail's nest   (c. 1952)

Female bowerbird's nest (c. 1900)

MUSEUM OF VICTORIA   (PHOTOGRAPH © DAVID SHEEHY)

Mudlark's nest

MUSEUM OF VICTORIA   (PHOTOGRAPH © DAVID SHEEHY)

John and Elizabeth Gould, satin bowerbird's nest   FROM *BIRDS OF AUSTRALIA*, VOL. IV   (PHOTOGRAPH © DAVID SHEEHY)

John and Elizabeth Gould, blue wrens and nest

FROM *BIRDS OF AUSTRALIA*, VOL. IV   (PHOTOGRAPH © DAVID SHEEHY)

trek across the Downs with their smooth hills and vistas of the sea. But instead of crossing the bridge at Southease, she stopped. The river, tidal and swollen with early spring rains, was flowing fast. Virginia put a stone in her pocket and clambered down the bank. She was a good swimmer and it must have been with great determination that she held herself beneath the water.

Does Woolf's final act undermine the hope and continuity symbolised by the swallows? There was a blackbird couple who lived in my neighbourhood, and one day the female (who is brown but still goes by the name blackbird) must have died. Perhaps she was hit by a car or taken by a predator. All day and every day for a week, the male perched on a nearby roof and called for her in such a frantic and heart-rending voice that it made me want to block my ears. His song of mourning, which was at first, *Where are you?*, and then became, *Why?*, and then became silence, was a tribute to all they'd accomplished together—the building of nests, the breeding and rearing of offspring and the intimacy of their active, attuned, productive relationship. He loved her (is that the right word?) and missed her. Maybe he later re-partnered. Blackbirds do. His elegy indicated that though a tragedy had occurred, some of its effects can be remedied by the effort of beauty. Perhaps also if another creature hears that song and understands that pain, then, by reading it, deciphering it, it can become a celebration.

When in 1954 the great Mexican artist Frida Kahlo, who was desperately ill and in agonising pain, completed her last work, a still life fecund with slices of juicy red watermelon, she titled it *Viva la vida*. Long live life.

The white stork was Karen Blixen's totem, an image of her life in story and reality. The bird's migration from Denmark to Kenya and back again symbolised Blixen's own journey, which was accompanied by similar perils and which resulted, thankfully, in a happy ending worthy of a fairytale. In Old and New World folklore, the white stork is associated with childbirth and good fortune. The large and graceful birds make enormous nests on the roofs or chimneys of houses to which they return year after year. To have a stork couple alight on your home and breed there is regarded as lucky. Perhaps the arrival of the storks in the spring was received with such gladness in northern Europe that it led to the birds being associated with birth and renewal, and to the popular image of a stork carrying a baby in its bill. Or maybe, in the days before sex education, when inquisitive children asked their parents where babies came from, the embarrassed parent could only think to stammer, 'The stork brought you!' For Blixen, the stork offered the possibility of seeing and understanding the pattern of her life, a vision she struggled to find in Africa and which she achieved, ironically, only after her grand failures there sent her on a humiliating return to Denmark. Where is home for the stork, where is its identity true, in Africa or Europe? The same question vexed Karen.

In 1913, Karen settled in Kenya where her husband, Count Bror von Blixen-Finecke, had purchased a large property on which they planned to grow coffee. In *Out of Africa*, her memoir of Kenya, she describes it as 'a landscape that had not its like in all the world. There was no fat on it and no luxuriance either; it was Africa distilled up through six thousand feet, like the strong and refined essence of a continent.' But, so high, it was unsuitable for growing coffee, making Karen's remark, 'We were never rich on the farm', something of an understatement.[18] The crop failed year after year, and even when it was capable of producing a harvest, the returns were minimal.

Her home, called Mbogani—Swahili for 'in the forest'—is today the Karen Blixen Museum in the suburb named after her on the outskirts of Nairobi. Karen told her mother how the nearby woods meant there was 'the most lovely bird song all around the house'. She was delighted to spot migratory birds from home: big flocks of swallows as well as storks 'that stroll about the meadows on the farm here just as if they were in a Danish marsh'.[19] Karen already felt connected to nature but in Africa a profound identification developed. 'The grass was me, and the air, the distant invisible mountains were me . . . I breathed with the slight night-wind in the thorntrees.'[20]

In 1914, Karen was diagnosed with syphilis, the result of Bror's philandering, and travelled home to Denmark for treatment. Though Karen confided in Thomas, her younger brother, she managed to keep the real nature of her illness a secret from the rest of her family. A bout of malaria, she informed her mother, required a change of air at home. After spending three months in hospital, where she was treated by leading venereologists, Karen was pronounced cured. But periods of illness—headaches, fevers and gastric ailments— dogged her for the rest of her life.

Karen met Denys Finch Hatton at Muthaiga Country Club in 1918, the watering hole of Kenya's colonial elite. Finch Hatton, the son of an earl, was an Oxford graduate. Debonair, witty and elusive, he was admired by all who knew him. He was a redoubtable hunter who made his living escorting wealthy tourists, including Edward, Prince of Wales, on safari. Muthaiga Country Club must be one of the most atmospheric places on earth. Entering, you walk straight into the 1920s. It's designed like an English gentlemen's club with a wood-panelled dining room where native Kenyans in white gloves discreetly serve the clientele an array of roasted meats with silver service, where afternoon tea is announced at four by a lightly rung gong and drinks are on the terrace. There's a stuffed lion in the hall, and when I stayed there in 2006 ladies were not allowed in the Gentlemen's Bar. Surrounded by well-tended grounds and guards toting rifles, Muthaiga remains an oasis of comfort in rough and ready Nairobi. It was *the* place to seduce Finch Hatton, infamous as it was for the riotous parties and reckless amours of the 'white mischief' set.

Karen pursued Denys with guile, charm and persistence, until he finally succumbed and moved into Mbogani. She and Bror had divorced, and Denys occupied Bror's old room. When Denys stayed at the farm, Karen declared, 'I have never been as happy, nor half as happy, in my life', because she was in the company of the 'most wonderful being on earth'. It was worth 'having lived and suffered, been ill, and had all the shauries [problems], to have lived for this week'.[21] When Denys departed, either to visit family in England or to go on safari, she slumped into depression, often retiring to bed for weeks. Karen shamelessly mythologised Denys in *Out of Africa*, eulogising him in inverse proportion to the amount of distress he caused her. Thus the ugly, messy, painful details of his comings and goings, the terror she experienced at his leave-takings, and his final abandonment of her are all erased.

By 1931, Karen was facing financial ruin. She appealed to Denys for help—he was on safari—but he could not offer enough cash, or did not wish to, and the property went on the market. Suffering from anaemia and dysentery, Karen was on the verge of a nervous collapse, eating and sleeping sporadically, her thoughts whirling. Sometimes at night she would rush out of the house and into the woods: 'I was driven out of my house by fear of losing it.' In a letter to her brother Thomas, she frankly canvassed the possibility of suicide. She was adamant she would not return to Denmark. It was 'quite out of the question . . . it would be completely and utterly unnatural for me'.[22]

Two things gave Karen unqualified pleasure during her last months in Kenya: Denys took her flying and she was rereading the tales of Hans Christian Andersen. While the rest of the world regarded him as a children's author, Denmark's best known writer was appreciated in his homeland for his sophisticated wit. Karen compared Andersen to Voltaire: he was 'a great magician' and his stories were 'some of the most edifying that have ever been written'.[23] Andersen's miserable personal life filled with rejections and unrequited love probably struck a chord with Karen, too. Andersen published his first stories in 1835 and died in 1875. His work captivated audiences in Denmark and abroad. As a child, Karen had been given a two-volume set of Andersen's tales. When her mother sent her a new copy, it was received with 'many, many thousand thanks', making her appreciate what 'a wonderful, delightful attribute imagination is,—indeed as I grow older I think it is truly divine, the foundation of everything else'.[24]

'The Storks' is a cautionary tale ending with a form of retribution usually associated with the Brothers Grimm. Like many 'fairytales', it's an ancient story derived from an oral tradition that Andersen popularised. On the roof of a house in a Danish village lives a stork family. The four young storks are terrified of a group of boys who taunt and threaten them. Only one child, Peter, refuses to join in, believing it's wrong to abuse animals. The pragmatic stork mother tries to dismiss the chicks' fears and beguiles them with the promise of the migration to Egypt with its heat and its abundance of food. But the young storks are afraid to try their wings in case they fall and the boys hurt them. The mother uses the problem as a spur. 'Do you want to freeze to death here when the winter comes?' she asks. 'Are the boys to come and hang you, and singe you, and roast you?'[25] Her words galvanise the young storks, who soon become adept flyers. But they swear revenge on the one boy who persists in tormenting them, and their mother agrees to help them.

She tells them about a pond 'in which all the little mortals lie until the stork comes and brings them to their parents. The pretty little babies lie there and dream more sweetly there than they ever dream afterwards.' In the pond, there is also 'a little dead child, one that has dreamed itself to death'; she says they will bring that one to the naughty boy, 'then he will cry because we have brought him a little dead brother'. Peter, the boy who refused to mock the storks, will receive 'a little brother and sister too'.[26] The moral of the story—that cruelty to animals doesn't pay—is tempered by the challenge that the boys provide: fearing them makes the young storks learn to fly, that is, to take on the challenges of maturity, with all its risks and potential for failure. Andersen draws little distinction between animals and humans: both are capable of cruelty and suffering. But the storks are more powerful, with agency over life and death. They can fly off, leaving the humans immured in winter where they 'sit in a dark room and cower', whereas the storks can 'fly about in foreign lands, where there are flowers and warm sunshine'.[27]

Was that how Karen thought of Denmark—as a place of imprisonment—while Africa meant freedom and pleasure? In *Out of Africa*, she recounts a story from her childhood which traced the stork's symbolism for her. While the story was being told to her, she explains, the storyteller drew a picture of a stork. Karen draws the same childlike sketch in *Out of Africa*. In the story, a man awakes in the night and hears a terrible noise. Investigating the noise, he stumbles over a rock, then into a ditch. He realises he was heading the wrong way and rushes off again in the opposite direction. Finally, after more injuries and confusion, he finds a leak in his dam and he sets to work to stop the hole and then returns to bed. When he awakes in the morning, he looks out his window and decides that the track of his wanderings around the property resembles the shape of a stork. The stork is a linear, visual representation of his journey, a map of his travails and his ultimate success. Karen was glad she had been told the story. 'I will remember it in my hour of need' because 'nothing made him turn around and go home, he finished his course, he kept his faith'.[28] His reward was to see the stork, the image of the fruition of his labours. Karen reflected, 'The tight place, the dark pit in which I am now lying, of what bird is it the talon? When the design of my life is completed, shall I, shall other people see a stork?'[29]

Karen had one more trial to undergo before she left Africa: in May 1931 Denys was killed in a plane crash near Nairobi. His funeral took place the following day, in the Ngong Hills at the commanding spot where he and Karen had chosen to be buried, which had a view of the farm. After the funeral, Karen tried to commit suicide by slashing her wrists but staunched the flow before she lost too much blood. Then she travelled home to Denmark.

Rungstedlund, Karen's family home, is approximately the same distance from Copenhagen as Mbogani is from Nairobi. The Danish house is by far the grander establishment. An imposing white two-storey, L-shaped building, it has forty acres of fields and woods spread behind it like a wide green cloak. The whole area now comprises the Karen Blixen Museet (Museum). In the warm months, the air is alive with birdsong. Swallows as well as woodpeckers, jackdaws, chaffinches and robins throng the trees. The storks, however, no longer visit. Pollution, it seems, is the reason they head further east each summer to make their homes.

Though she felt wretched, Karen was finally in a protective place that relieved her of gruelling responsibilities. The proofs of Rungstedlund's abiding peace and inspiration are manifest in the quality and quantity of Karen's publications. Between 1934 and her death in 1962 she published a novel, four collections of short stories and two works of non-fiction, as well as giving lectures and readings and, towards the end of her life, a series of popular radio broadcasts from the living room. Karen came back to Rungstedlund an abject failure, and died there an internationally renowned figure, regarded as one of the country's major writers. *Out of Africa*, published in 1937, was an immediate international bestseller, making Karen a celebrity, which she adored. Ernest Hemingway thought it should have won the Nobel Prize for literature. The ravages of syphilis and increasing ill-health made Karen skeletally thin. She had enormous kohl-ringed eyes that shone like black diamonds, her admirers recalled. She dressed with drama and elegance, creating an impression of gothic chic, and survived on a diet of oysters, champagne and amphetamines.

The migration of homo sapiens to Europe that occurred about seventy thousand years ago is known as the 'Out of Africa' model. Africa is the birthplace of our species, where we came down from the trees, leaving the birds there, where we evolved as humans around two hundred thousand years ago. It's where we developed our big brain, twice the size of our nearest genetic relative the chimpanzee; our thumb, so important for gripping; and our big toe that enabled us to walk upright. It's where we began to make tools and develop language. The Out of Africa model is supported by archaeological evidence with several important finds gleaned from Kenya's Rift Valley. I think Karen would be delighted to know that her book, in which she told and, by telling, understood her own journey, has been used to name humanity's first and most crucial one.

Karen wanted to make one last noble gesture—to protect Rungstedlund and create a wildlife reserve—but she did not have sufficient capital. In a radio talk in 1958, she told her audience that she had

> come to look upon Rungstedlund as belonging particularly to the migratory birds . . . The seasons here are first and foremost characterised by their arrivals and departures. How many times have I not, in the nights around the spring or autumnal equinox, stood outside the house and listened to their flight high in the heavens above the roof!

She hoped the property could become 'a true paradise for birds which have come here over the oceans of the world'.[30]

And how many times had Karen watched the storks return to their nests or build new ones? The stork's nest is a massive structure which can grow to over two metres in diameter and about three metres in depth. Storks return to the same nest each year, adding to it. They begin with a broad twig platform and then slowly, carefully and faultlessly build upwards and outwards. The white stork commonly nests on roofs and chimneys but sometimes it chooses trees, church steeples, overhead powerlines or telephone poles, the higher the better. What looks perilous is as solid as rock.

Because of the affection that humans have developed for storks, in some places we've sought to help by building structures for them such as platforms on rooftops or special nest towers. The white stork is the emblem of Lithuania and you'd be hard pressed to find folk more enthusiastic about storks than the people of its capital Vilnius. The Lithuanian Ornithological Society declared 2010 the year of the white stork and to celebrate the citizens of Vilnius decided to build a huge nest, twenty metres square. As the Society's website puts it, 'Everyone can go in it and feel like a little stork.'[31] Its construction was timed to welcome the storks back from their journey to Africa. On the nest platform, recorded stork sounds could be heard. Storks don't sing or trill like most birds but clatter their beaks; it sounds rather like clapping.

An issue for storks, and for many other big migratory birds like the osprey, is the destruction of their habitat. With financial support from the European Union, the Lithuanian Ornithological Society has assisted in rebuilding more than three thousand nests and it has also raised five hundred artificial platforms for the birds. You can buy one of these specially designed wooden platforms online from the Society's website to erect in your yard. It looks like a piece of furniture from Ikea, though one hopes it is easier to wrangle. In Australia, we have only one member of the stork family, a Black-necked stork. Though it doesn't migrate, its nest resembles those of its northern hemisphere relatives. In April 2010, the people of Vilnius organised a festival in the storks' honour, which included a concert and a theatre performance. The website notes, 'they will also vote "Storks against cabbage"—vote, what is true: storks bring children or they are found in cabbage . . . Visitors also can take the quiz "Do you know stork?" and a photoshoot "I am stork."'[32] The legs of migratory birds are ringed to track their travels. For the fun of it, three hundred residents of Vilnius wore a ring of tape around their ankles, which was commemorated in the 'I am stork' photoshoot. The children loved it, of course, and the artificial nest was full of 'climbing children.'[33]

With the talons of an owl and the vision of an eagle, the osprey is among the most successful hunters among raptors.

Wildlife photographer Andy Rouse admires how the osprey hunts, the way it 'powers into the water like a falling brick, creating an enormous splash'. Arising from the water, it looks completely dazed but then 'turns into the wind and erupts into the air', usually with a struggling fish in its talons.[34] The osprey's wingspan measures two metres and it makes a nest every bit as fabulous and huge as the stork's. New York's Long Island plays host to the birds when they return from their journey to South America: Brazil is a favourite destination. In the 1950s and 60s, their numbers began to decline due to the use of the pesticide DDT and loss of habitat due to urbanisation, and the osprey went on the endangered species list. But when DDT was banned in the US in 1972, after public concern generated by Rachel Carson's book *Silent Spring*, the osprey's numbers soon increased. The locals on Long Island got involved and started building platforms for the birds to replace the trees that had been cut down. Clearly, the evolutionary drive means that the osprey doesn't give a damn whether it creates its nest in a tree or a human-made structure. Its survival now seems assured.

Karen's interest in the migratory birds incited her to save Rungstedlund as she had been unable to save the African farm. In her radio broadcast, she asked her audience to contribute one krone each to a foundation that would administer the estate, while she would donate all future royalties from her books.

The public response was generous, enthusiastic and gratifying, a tribute to the esteem in which she was held, and in a short time a substantial sum was raised to administer Rungstedlund. Two days before Karen's death, Thomas Dinesen sat beside his sister's bed. 'Do you find it strange,' she asked him, 'when I tell you that I have lived a most happy life?'[35] Karen is buried beneath the boughs of a magnificent beech tree on the estate and so, fittingly, she rests with the birds.

5
The poetry of nests

PLAGUED AS I AM WITH insomnia, there's no hour of the night that is unfamiliar to me. There are benefits. I've heard the vixen's weird, erotic cry. The hiss of a possum can sound so furious, loud and unearthly (especially if the possum has taken up residence in your roof) it could be Beelzebub himself. I've also heard the nightingale. With friends, I'd driven down to Provence from Paris and we were staying in the hills behind Cannes. Everyone else in the house was asleep when, in the pre-dawn stillness, a bird began to sing in such a piercingly beautiful voice it went straight to my heart. There's nothing to compare to the nightingale because its song is unlike any other bird's, and its allure all the more compelling because the male delivers his song at full volume in darkness. It was breeding season and he was singing for a mate who, apparently, required as little sleep as he.

To poor John Keats, spluttering with tuberculosis at his home near Hampstead Heath, the nightingale's song was an invitation to 'cease upon the midnight with no pain'. Perhaps it's no surprise that to Keats the nightingale's glorious voice occasioned thoughts of 'easeful Death'. In 1819, when Keats wrote 'Ode to a Nightingale', he was twenty-four and had less than two years to live. His poetry was largely reviled by the critics (Lord Byron believed the bad reviews finished Keats off) and he was dependent for money and shelter on the kindness of his friends. He was besotted with Fanny Brawne, a spirited and intelligent young woman, but marriage, and pretty much anything else, was out of the question. As Percy Bysshe Shelley commented in 'To a Skylark', the 'sweetest songs are those that tell of saddest thought'.

Keats and Shelley were friends, though Keats had reservations about Shelley's radical views and penchant for scandalous behaviour. Shelley was also a toff and Keats was low-born, and Keats had a chip on his shoulder about the upper classes. Byron might have been regarded as mad, bad and dangerous to know but Shelley was equally wild. When Shelley fell in love with Mary Godwin in 1814, she was nearly seventeen and he five years older. Mary was the daughter of the social reformers and philosophers William Godwin and Mary Wollstonecraft

(Wollstonecraft had died after giving birth to Mary). Shelley was an admirer of their views and he was a visitor to Godwin's home. At the time they met, Shelley was already married and he and Mary caused an outrage by running off to the Continent, only to return to England when Mary discovered she was pregnant. In 1816, Harriet, Shelley's wife, drowned herself in the Serpentine River in London, giving Mary and Shelley the opportunity to marry. But, ostracised from polite society, the Shelleys returned to Italy. Earlier in 1816, while holidaying with Byron near Geneva, Mary had conceived of *Frankenstein*, her major work, which was published two years later. In Italy, the Shelleys lived an itinerant existence and were part of cultured expatriate communities. Though both were productive, Mary was despondent, owing to the death of three infants and Shelley's proclivity for flirting with women close to her.

In 1820, hearing of Keats' deteriorating health, Shelley invited him to stay at the Shelleys' residence at Pisa. Keats needed to escape another English winter. He was touched by Percy's offer, recognising that the Shelleys were financially strapped. Shelley looked forward to the visit, writing:

> I shall take care to bestow every possible attention on [Keats]. I consider his a most valuable life, & I am deeply interested in his safety. I intend to be physician both of his body & of

his soul, to keep the one warm & to teach [the] other Greek
& Spanish. I am aware indeed in part, that I am nourishing
a rival who will far surpass [me] and this is an additional
motive & will be an added pleasure.[1]

However, other well-meaning friends had arranged for Keats
to travel to Rome, where, due to a series of misadventures
and his own worsening condition, he died early in 1821. To
honour his friend and assuage his own grief, Shelley wrote
'Adonais, an Elegy on the Death of John Keats'. Adonis, the
symbol of masculine beauty, was a Greek youth beloved of
the goddesses Aphrodite and Persephone, who vied for his
favours. Mick Jagger read part of 'Adonais' at Brian Jones'
memorial concert in London's Hyde Park in July 1969. It was a
fitting tribute from the reckless young romantics of the 1960s
to their cultural forebears.

'To a Skylark' was composed in June 1820 when Shelley was
twenty-seven. He was taking a stroll one evening with Mary
when he heard the bird singing. Given the disasters that beset
Shelley and Mary, it is to Shelley's credit that he managed to
release his own poetry with such unguarded emotion, in an
ecstatic voice similar to the one he admired in the skylark.
Two years later, Shelley drowned in a boating accident at La
Spezia, near Livorno. Several of the Romantic poets died young
and tragically, after completing, in the case of both Shelley

and Keats, oeuvres of sumptuous and immortal verse. Most particularly, they revelled in nature.

Neither the skylark nor the nightingale are glamorous birds—they're both brown and rather dull looking. Skylarks were introduced into Australia by homesick English folk in the 1850s and 60s. It was a success, unlike the introduction of nightingales, who decided the Australian climate was not for them. At the Melbourne Museum, I examined the skylark's nest. The bird densely weaves grasses to make a nest about fifteen centimetres across and whose walls are about the width of my index finger. Its location seems rash: the skylark doesn't bother with trees or even a bush but constructs the nest on the ground in moist pastures or short-grassed fields. Golf links are favoured these days. 'From the earth thou springest,' observed Shelley. Attaching a nest to a branch is a tricky business, but at least it's fixed. Making a nest on the ground means that until the nest is heavy enough to resist gravity it can shift.

The males have a song flight for which they are justly famous, as my *Reader's Digest Guide to Australian Birds* tells me. Rising on quivering wings, they ascend almost vertically for up to a hundred metres, singing a continuous medley of rippling trills, and stay aloft for many minutes before sinking and dropping silently to the ground, wings closed. To Shelley, the skylark was an image of 'unbodied joy', its 'profuse strains . . . unpremeditated art'. In fact, towards the poem's end, Shelley becomes rather envious. The bird's skill was 'Better than all treasures/That in books are found'. Indeed, the skylark was a poet who could perhaps teach Shelley its gladness, its 'clear keen joyance' denied to melancholic humans who reflect on 'love's sad satiety' and who 'pine for what is not'.

It was perhaps a skylark's nest that was found by one of Robert Frost's children and recorded in his poem 'The Exposed Nest', written in 1920. I did try to find some happy poets but largely without success. Perhaps those who sought transcendence in nature used it as a recourse from their miserable lives. Robert Frost's father died when the boy was eleven, leaving the family broke. In 1900, his mother died. In 1920, Robert had to commit his younger sister Jeanie to an asylum where she died nine years later. In 1895, Robert married Elinor Miriam White and they had six children. Their first son, Elliott, died of cholera when he was three. Their second son committed suicide. Their second daughter Irma went mad and, in her forties, was placed in an asylum. A third daughter died in childbirth aged nineteen, while the fourth and youngest daughter died just three days after her birth. Lesley, the eldest girl, who was born in 1899, lived to a ripe old age. Robert himself lived until he was eighty-eight and, as America's unofficial poet laureate, was awarded four Pulitzer Prizes, as well as honorary degrees too numerous to mention.

A highlight of Frost's life was reading his verse at the 1961 presidential inauguration of John F. Kennedy in Washington.

I'm not sure which of Frost's ill-starred children was the one who was described in 'The Exposed Nest' as 'forever finding some new play'. In a meadow 'busy with the new-cut hay', the child finds a nest full of young birds which 'the cutter bar had just gone champing over/(Miraculously without tasting flesh)'. The child—I'm guessing it's a girl—wants to restore the nest to its former hiding place and her father seeks to help. Frost, a knowledgeable observer of nature, wonders if the mother bird will care for the chicks after such a change of scene. Might human meddling make the female abandon the nest? Not to disappoint his child, Frost aids her in building a screen and giving the nestlings back their protection and shade. 'We saw the risk we took in doing good,/But dared not spare to do the best we could'. The poem ends flatly. There was 'no more to tell . . . We turned to other things.' Frost has no memory of returning to the nest site to see 'if the birds lived the first night through,/And so at last to learn to use their wings.'

Given the almost ceaseless flow of personal tragedy that engulfed Frost's life, it's no wonder that he's ambivalent about restoring the nest. 'All this to prove we cared' is rather like a shrug of the shoulders. *You do your best but . . .* The child has optimism and resolve while the father—who is wise in bird lore but who has also been defeated, time and again, by his attempts to save his own children—is more cautious. Some of Frost's children gained adulthood, learned to 'use their wings', only to be struck down by illness, either physical or mental. The death of a child must be every parent's nightmare, and if it occurs, a waking nightmare.

Frost's famous poem 'Stopping by Woods on a Snowy Evening' was written two years after 'The Exposed Nest'. It broods on death. The narrator has paused by a forest on the 'darkest evening of the year', the winter solstice, the shortest day, just before Christmas. While his horse must think it's odd 'to stop without a farmhouse near', the narrator offers no explanation. He's mesmerised by the woods which are 'lovely, dark and deep'. But he recalls he has 'promises to keep'. Then comes the hypnotic refrain, 'And miles to go before I sleep,/ And miles to go before I sleep.' Without commitments (to home? to family?), he might walk into the snowy darkness of the forest and never return. Had Frost himself, also given to depression, contemplated such a fate near Christmas, a time devoted to children and to family, resplendent with the symbol of the Christ child, of hope and renewal?

In Emily Dickinson's poem 'For every Bird a Nest', she celebrates the skylark both for its modesty and its song. Dickinson, with her dark, bright, intense eyes, described herself as 'small, like the wren'.[2] In another poem Dickinson comments, '"Hope" is the thing with feathers—/That perches in the soul'. During her life, the reclusive American poet published only a few of her nearly 1800 works. After Dickinson's death in 1886, the trove was discovered by her sister Lavinia, and subsequently published. It aroused immediate interest. Since 1955, when a scholarly edition of the poems finally appeared, Dickinson's reputation has grown and she is now considered one of America's finest poets.

'For every Bird a Nest', written in 1859, contrasts the ambitions of the wren and the skylark, and draws moral parallels. The wren searches for a place to build her nest but, with 'households in every tree', it proves difficult. The proud wren has aristocratic ambitions: she wants to build up high with 'fine twigs' while the skylark 'is not ashamed/To build upon the ground/Her modest house'. Then Dickinson asks,

> Yet who of all the throng
> Dancing around the sun
> Does so rejoice?

It's reminiscent of the passage from the gospel of Matthew: 'Look at the birds of the air; they neither sow nor reap nor gather into barns, and yet your heavenly Father feeds them.'

What did a nest mean to Dickinson? It's an image to which she returned. A year earlier than 'For every Bird a Nest', she'd written a poem about birds, nests, sisters and home: 'One Sister have I in our house,/And one, a hedge away.' 'Both belong to me,' Dickinson comments. Susan Gilbert Dickinson was Emily's beloved friend and sister-in-law, who lived next door—a hedge away—while Dickinson shared her home with her younger sister, Lavinia. I mean beloved quite literally because Emily, who did not marry, worshipped Sue, the 'Only Woman in the World'.[3] It was a lasting and a troubled love, recorded in scores of Dickinson's notes, letters and provocative lyrics. 'Susan—I would have come out of Eden to open the Door for you if I had known you were there,' Dickinson writes six years before her death.[4] Biographer Judith Farr has memorably described Sue as 'the central radiance' of Emily's emotional life.[5]

Emily had encouraged her older brother Austin to marry Sue, presumably so she could keep Sue close, and he underwent a three-year courtship before, rather unwillingly it seems, Sue agreed. She was a complex woman, at times tempestuous and outspoken, at others coolly detached. She craved social prominence, and all the prestige and finery that went with it, yet she was capricious enough to throw rowdy parties which shocked the Puritan townsfolk of Amherst, Massachusetts. They were alternately charmed and alienated by Sue, who was smart, adventurous and sophisticated. Her marriage to Austin deteriorated: he conducted a very public affair while she courted gossip by flirting with the dashing editor of the local newspaper.

Emily's bid to secure Sue's place in her life was built on ambiguity and pain. After the birth of Sue's children, she distanced herself from Emily, to the poet's anguish. Perhaps Sue could not cope with Emily's desperate, illicit needs. It's unlikely the affair was ever consummated, and themes of renunciation and solitude haunt Dickinson's verse. But Emily's passion for Sue inspired her poetry, the cryptically encoded love poems which Dickinson sent her.

In 'One Sister have I in our house', Dickinson welcomes Sue into the family circle. Sue was the bird who 'builded' her nest in the Dickinsons' hearts. Emily recalls their early friendship, their 'Childhood', where she held Sue's hand 'the tighter—/Which shortened all the miles'. The poem ends with the exultant cry: 'Sue—forevermore!' In the letters addressed to Sue during their young womanhood, Emily sees the two as birds, mounting together on wings of love. 'I move on wings now, Susie, on wings as white as snow, and as bright as summer sunshine—because I am with you.'[6] In another poem, Dickinson writes,

> Her breast is fit for pearls,
> But I was not a 'Diver'—
> Her brow is fit for thrones
> But I have not a crest.
> Her heart is fit for *home*—

I—a Sparrow—build there
Sweet of twigs and twine
My perennial nest.

Though Sue, worthy of being a queen, deserves nothing but the best—'pearls' and 'thrones'—Emily wasn't a 'Diver'—a man, presumably. She was without 'a crest'. Crest has a sexual connotation—the cock's comb or the erect plume of a soldier's helmet. Did Emily believe she had failed Sue by being a woman? Dickinson then retreats from erotic metaphors to consider Sue's true desire, her heart's needs—a *home* (Dickinson's emphasis). Emily describes herself as a sparrow, that cheerful, small and humble bird, who will build in Sue's heart, 'sweet of twigs and twine', an enduring nest, a safe place, a place for *her*. Emily may not be able to provide pearls for Sue's breast (an image of sensuality) or thrones for her noble brow (a reference to Sue's public life) but she can offer a domestic, less exalted sphere. By encouraging her brother to marry Sue, who had no means and who was supporting herself by teaching, Dickinson helped provide the security that Sue craved.

The nest as home was a crucial image for Dickinson, who gradually retreated from the world to tend her garden, write her masterpieces and endure her private agonies and ecstasies. If friends or relatives came to visit, she sent a polite note, explaining she could not see them, while she sat upstairs in her room. When Emily died at fifty-five, most who knew her had not seen her face for a quarter of a century. She did not even permit her doctor to examine her: the closest he got was to glimpse her fully dressed figure pass an open doorway, her face averted. Sue provided Emily's most intimate final service: she washed and dressed the body for burial. She did not attend Emily's funeral but wrote a stirring and perceptive obituary for the local paper, the first tribute to Dickinson's talent: 'Her swift poetic rapture was like the long glistening note of a bird one hears in the June woods at high noon, but can never see.'[7]

John Clare, a contemporary of Keats, wrote finely observed studies of nests. Promoted by his publishers as 'the peasant poet', Clare was born in the village of Helpston in Cambridgeshire. He had scant education, though he loved words and poetry from an early age. He was always scribbling, much to the disgust of his mother, who regularly destroyed his verses if she found them. Clare's true learning derived from the natural environment, for which he held a religious reverence—'I always wrote my poems in the fields'.[8] That was also where he worked: Clare was a casual labourer, tending sheep or horses, scaring birds from the grain, weeding. Later he became a gardener and a lime burner. But any kind of continuous work—or pressure—did not suit him, and nor did the disruption of leaving his part of the world. Departures provoked nervous breakdowns, perhaps the result of manic depression. Clare's parents, like the rest of the village, considered him crazy and they were rather ashamed of John until he found success with his first book, *Poems, Descriptive of Rural Life and Scenery*, published in 1820.

In 'The Nightingale's Nest', Clare informs me, the ignorant naturalist, that the female sings as well as the male 'at morn, at eve, nay, all the live-long day' as though 'she lived on song'. Though Clare greatly admired Keats—the two corresponded but did not meet—Clare felt that Keats was hampered by his lack of direct contact with nature: '[Keats'] descriptions of scenery are often very fine but as it is the case with other inhabitants of great cities he often described nature as she appeared to his fancies and not as he would have described her had he witnessed the things he described'.[9] When Clare published 'The Nightingale's Nest' in his second volume of poems, *The Rural Muse*, in 1835, he was a better known poet than Keats.

Jonathan Bate, Clare's biographer, deems 'The Nightingale's Nest' the supreme work in *The Rural Muse*. Writing in the present tense, Clare invites the audience to accompany him as he searches for the nest. 'Hush!' warns Clare, we must tread quietly or our noise might drive the nightingale from her 'home of love'. Since he was a boy, Clare had been coming to this precise spot 'and watched her while she sung'. Clare shares his surprise with us—fancy that 'so famed a bird/Should have no better dress than russet brown'! But it's her voice that counts. He recalls how her wings trembled in 'her ecstasy', her mouth opened wide 'to release her heart/Of its out-sobbing songs'. But Clare had to be careful—a slight movement and she'd be gone. Remembering this, he gently parts the hazel branches near a dense blackthorn thicket, where 'rude boys never think to look', until, suddenly, 'as I live! her secret nest is here'. But the nightingale has heard him. She flits away to a nearby oak bough, 'mute in her fears' that she might betray her home. But Clare wishes only to observe, not to destroy. He admires the nest, which is unlike any other bird's—loosely woven from 'dead oaken leaves' while within it has a velvety softness. There are also little scraps of grass and 'down and hair'. The 'hermit's mossy cell' snugly holds five olive-brown eggs. 'So here we'll leave them,' announces Clare, closing the magical moment, 'still unknown to wrong'.

For the last twenty years of his life, Clare was incarcerated in a madhouse. His mood swings had worsened, he was subject to delusions (at times he thought he was Byron, at others, a sea captain or a champion boxer) and his periodic fits of violence meant his wife and children could no longer cope with him. Fortunately for Clare, it was an enlightened madhouse where the inmates were treated with a degree of respect, but for a man whose source of inspiration—and whose very being—depended on his connection with nature's freedom it was a sad fate.

Clare's final poem, 'Birds Nests', was written in 1863. It's a reverie, as well as a portrait and a memory of the landscape. It's spring and 'warm glows the South'. Clare observes a chaffinch carrying moss in its beak as it builds a nest in a hazel hedge. The bird charms the poet 'with his beautiful song'. Bleak winds may blow across the marshes but in Clare's little nook 'warm the sunshines'. Completing the idyllic picture is an old cow contentedly chewing her cud. God's in his heaven and all's right with the world—though Clare has just scratched his last poem onto a sheet of foolscap with a shaky hand, six months before his death.

•

Recently, I found a nest. Actually, I didn't find it, someone else did and carefully placed it on a fence in a neighbouring street and I brought it home with me. I think it's a sparrow's nest, so perhaps I won't have to turn it in to the Department of Sustainability and Environment. Sparrows are not a protected species but I'm concerned that a diligent officer from the department, after reading this chapter, might come knocking on my door to verify my claim.

I would be loath to hand it over. It's a superb creation, though a little the worse for wear. The rim has worn away; this occurs when the chicks grow and, in their eagerness to be fed by their returning parents, outreach the edge and wear it down. (I watched the process with a family of noisy miners who lived up the canal. Noisy miners resemble common mynas with their yellow eye-bands, but they're native birds and they have bright yellow bills and grey feathers. The adults built the nest in low branches, which meant I could comfortably watch the action from a fence post. As the nestlings grew, their increasing size and energy, as well as their constant pushing against the nest edge, gradually unravelled it. At first the parents rebuilt the edge—probably concerned the babies could fall out—but gave up as the chicks grew bigger. Within a week, the birds had fledged and I next saw them as young adults, perching on the lower branches of the same tree, still asking for, and receiving, food from their parents.)

Around the sparrow's nest, the bird has arranged (for fun? for decoration?) a white and now rather grubby ribbon, giving it the air of a gift. I've placed the nest on a low table in the living room with some of my other treasures. There's a hunk of glistening rose quartz rivered with milky-coloured skeins. A leaf skeleton that I found in the street and framed. A mosasaur's tooth. (The mosasaur—the T-Rex of the sea—lived 65 million years ago and grew to be up to seventeen metres long. A particularly fierce predator, it had two sets of teeth, one in its mouth and one set running down the centre of its throat, so for its prey once caught there was no chance of escape.) The fossil—the tooth is embedded in stone—comes from the coast of Morocco, the mosasaur's former haunt. Next to the tooth I've arranged three ammonite fossils, a squid with a shell that the mosasaurs found delectable and which are perfect, shiny brown spirals. There's a lachrymatorium, a small, slender-necked Roman vase made of green iridescent glass, probably from the first century AD. Roman wives gave the lachrymatorium—literally 'tear vessel'—to their husbands on their return from battle with the barbarians or from building Hadrian's Wall or whatever other epic task the Roman legions were engaged in. So the legend goes, the lachrymatorium held the tears which the wife had shed in her husband's absence. A large vase is filled with sea-washed glass and shells collected from Long Island, the Italian Riviera, Apollo Bay, Key West and other beaches that I've forgotten. Next to it is a goblet where I've arranged birds' feathers like flowers.

William Wordsworth describes the thrill of finding a sparrow's nest within 'the leafy shade' at his father's home in the Lakes District in north-west England. Wordsworth was startled when he spied the sparrow's 'home and shelter'd bed'. The nest contained three bright blue eggs that 'gleam'd like a vision'. It was a discovery he shared with his sister, called Emmeline in the poem, actually Wordsworth's younger sister Dorothy, his muse and companion. The poem, written in 1801, is a tribute to her. Both were children when they found the nest—Dorothy was 'a little Prattler among men'—but she was imbued with such tenderness, 'such heart was in her', that she became 'the blessing' of Wordsworth's later years.

> She gave me eyes, she gave me ears;
> And humble cares, and delicate fears;
> A heart, the fountain of sweet tears;
>   And love, and thought, and joy.

William, who was born in 1770, was one year older than Dorothy. With Ann and John, their parents, and three other siblings, all boys, they lived at Cockermouth on the River Derwent. Wordsworth's earliest memories dwell on the 'giddy bliss' offered to a child by a house whose garden was bordered by the 'alder shades and rocky falls' of the river.[10] At the end of the garden, Wordsworth recalled, was a high terrace that commanded views of the Derwent and Cockermouth Castle. It was the children's favourite playground. The terrace wall was covered with a closely clipped privet hedge and climbing roses, giving an almost impervious shelter to nesting birds. It remained an enchanted realm for Wordsworth.

Part of William and Dorothy's mutual devotion was founded on their loss of one another, as children, for nearly a decade. The family split apart in 1778 when Ann contracted pneumonia and died. William boarded at school while Dorothy went to live with relatives. Further calamity befell the children in 1783 when their father died. After settling the estate, it was discovered that John's former employer, the powerful and cantankerous Lord Lonsdale, owed John several thousand pounds. Lonsdale refused to settle and the Wordsworth family had no option but to pursue the matter through the courts. The Wordsworth children's guardians—two uncles—grudgingly took responsibility for their charges. While William attended school and, during term, had the good fortune to board with a kindly family, Dorothy had no such escape. At the home of her uncle Christopher, she was constantly scolded and the servants were insolent to her, rightly judging, 'how they may treat dependants who ought to be grateful not proud'.[11]

In 1787, William and Dorothy were reunited for a summer which they spent rambling through the countryside. It was the first time they'd been together in nearly a decade. Dorothy, now sixteen, had grown into a sensitive and imaginative young woman. Wordsworth cherished her: 'Now, after separation desolate,/Restored to me—such absence that she seemed/A gift then first bestowed.'[12] The two often discussed their miserable and frustrating circumstances, 'wishing', as Dorothy commented, 'we had a father and a home'.[13] Wordsworth was preparing to study at Cambridge but Dorothy had to return to a place where she was certain she was not wanted. She looked, rather desperately, to the future where 'my Brother fired with the idea of leading his sister to such a retreat as Fancy ever ready at our call hastens to assist us in painting' will take her to a home of their own.[14]

Their wish came true. After receiving a legacy from a friend, Wordsworth was in a position to invite Dorothy to the tranquil and picturesque setting of Grasmere in the Lakes District, where they lived for the rest of their lives. Dorothy managed the home for William, as well as accompanying him on long walks, reading his poetry, offering valuable criticism and providing a steady and inspiring focus; she also wrote a journal which contained her observations on nature, and Wordsworth found these invaluable. She was certainly as important an influence on him as his great friend Samuel Taylor Coleridge. 'Home at Grasmere', a poem Wordsworth wrote when they first settled there, celebrates the return to the childhood realm, his true 'abiding place', which is made all the more important because of Dorothy.

> Her voice was like a hidden Bird that sang;
> The thought of her was like a flash of light
> Or an unseen companionship, a breath
> Of fragrance independent of the wind.

In 1802, Wordsworth married Mary Hutchinson, a childhood friend, who was also devoted to Dorothy. Mary and William had five children, and Dorothy was their practical and affectionate aunt. But she wasn't a doormat: she negotiated strenuously and successfully for a stipend from her uncle so she was not beholden to William and Mary for her keep.

Poems in Two Volumes, which was published in 1807, and which contained 'The Sparrow's Nest', had a disastrous reception. Byron, all of nineteen, led the attack: he savaged *Poems*, describing the bulk of the verses as puerile, commonplace and namby-pamby. Time has dimmed the fury which greeted *Poems* and which seems incomprehensible now. Included were some of Wordsworth's best-remembered works, such as 'Daffodils' and 'The Solitary Reaper'. Perhaps expectations, after the fame Wordsworth had garnered for *Tintern Abbey* in 1798, were simply too high. I first read 'The Sparrow's Nest' in a book of collected verse for schoolchildren titled *Foothills of Poetry*, which I've kept all these years. Its nature poetry was my introduction to Wordsworth, Yeats, Tennyson and Andrew Marvell. Frost's 'Stopping by Woods on a Snowy Evening' is in there, too. In my careful, twelve-year-old hand with my inky-nibbed pen, I copied Wordsworth's 'The Rainbow' on the opening page.

'The Sparrow's Nest' impressed me because of its sentimentality, the worshipful way that Wordsworth credited his younger sister with literally making him human, with giving him vision ('eyes'), humility ('humble cares') and sensibility ('delicate fears'), as well as the ability to feel and to weep—and to not be ashamed of weeping ('A heart, the fountain of sweet tears'). Dorothy as the feminine also offers the ability to love fully, to be intellectually engaged and, finally—and most importantly, it seems—to experience joy. For Wordsworth, these are the ingredients for a stimulating and fulfilling existence.

Wordsworth took the nest from his memory and, by writing about it, placed it in the present. It's an optimistic act: the nest, the true 'abiding place', can be recovered and restored, and what was good and useful about the past can take a productive role in the present. Wordsworth's home, his family circle that included Mary, Dorothy and the children, radiated happiness, as its many visitors attested. But even fairytales must come to an end. By 1835, Dorothy had developed dementia and William and Mary tended her during her long decline. Wordsworth died in 1850, Dorothy five years later and Mary in 1859. They are buried together in the graveyard at Grasmere. A happy ending. More or less.

6
What is art?

At a certain point in human history, our attitude towards animals altered. The Lascaux cave painters in south-western France, who hunted huge bison, pictured them as glorious beasts, alert and energetic, worthy of reverence and admiration, even though the bison (and the other animals the men hunted) could cause terrible injuries and death. These paintings were done in the Paleolithic era, more than 17,000 years ago. Much to the amusement of the Romans, who considered such beliefs bizarre, the Egyptians worshipped animals; their serene, enigmatic gods wore the heads of cats or crocodiles. The scarab beetle, its image festooned on jewellery, coffins and obelisks, was the Egyptians' emblem of resurrection and eternal life. The scarab patiently rolls its dung into balls, then deposits them in underground tunnels; there the female buries the larvae in the dung balls. When the young are born, they consume the dung and emerge 'magically' from beneath the sand. It's a nature-respecting culture that can find a potent symbol in such a humble creature.

During the era of the pagan civilisations, it seemed that humans continued to offer animals an honoured place within culture, even though urban settlement and the cultivation of land meant humanity was no longer dependent on them for food. I'm not suggesting that pagans were especially kind to animals: the appalling cruelty meted out to thousands of wild creatures in the games at the Colosseum in Rome puts paid to such a notion. There were pagan cults, too, where animals were brutally sacrificed to a particular deity, to the bloodthirsty cheers of worshippers. The Egyptians also developed some ghastly customs. Domestic cats, worshipped as the personification of the goddess Bastet, were sacrificed, mummified and entombed in their thousands at Bastet's chief temple at Bubastis. To keep up with demand, the Egyptians established cat islands on the Nile where the cats were bred purely for slaughter.

In Ovid's *Metamorphoses*—a collection of Greek myths about transformation—the poetic boundaries between the human, animal and divine worlds are liminal. A Roman poet writing at the beginning of the last millennium, Ovid recognised that the gods were fickle and that our animal nature could re-emerge at any moment. There's usually a moral to the stories. Arachne, with 'insane audacity', challenged the goddess Athena to a weaving contest.[1] Arachne's expert tapestry showed the gods' misdemeanours: in one scene she depicted Zeus, who had an eye for the ladies, pursuing Europa in the guise of a bull to have his way with her. Athena was furious and tore the tapestry to pieces; she then changed Arachne into a spider. 'She yet spins her thread,' writes Ovid, 'and as a spider is as busy with her web as of old.'[2]

Judaic monotheism, adopted by Christianity, has at its core the creation myth recorded in the book of Genesis, the story that God created the world in six days for the benefit of man. In the early centuries of the last millennium, the rise of Christianity in the West crushed pagan civilisation. It placed man at the top of the ladder and everything in creation was below him. Ovid was popular but the early Christian teachers and preachers disapproved; indeed they banned pagan writers, especially the poets, as likely to be harmful to the morals of the reader. From their point of view, Ovid's writings with their frank tales of the Olympians' lusty and extravagant behaviour were calculated to do much harm, however charming they might seem. As Mary M. Innes, a translator of *Metamorphoses*, notes, 'their charm made them all the more dangerous'.[3] Ovid was reintroduced into Western civilisation in the fourteenth

century when Dante described him in *The Divine Comedy* as
the third most important pagan poet after Homer and Horace.
That was at the beginning of the Renaissance, whose central
stimulus was the rediscovery of classical civilisation and its
application, most notably, to art and architecture.

While European folktales, like those of Hans Christian
Andersen, preserved the magical role of animals in human
welfare, by the nineteenth century these were designated as
'fairytales', bedtime stories for children. In India, however,
where polytheism has continued, animals remain objects
of reverence. Sacred cows wander casually through Delhi's
congested streets. At the Galta Temple near Jaipur in northern
India, the monkeys have their own temple, which is dedi-
cated to the ape god, Hanuman. Indigenous people, such as
Australian Aboriginal tribes, maintain vital connections with
totemic animals through seasonal, ceremonial ritual.

Have cultural shifts led to a disbelief in the abilities and the
intelligence of animals, a lack of imagination regarding what
smart animals can and have achieved? We can't expect the
animals to tell us. As Nathan Emery comments, 'We will never
be able to find human theory of mind in nonhumans. They
have their own social cognition that has evolved for their own
problems.'[4] Nicky Clayton is aware that the predominant attitude of Western science has been that animals are unthinking
automatons until proved otherwise, in line with the biblical

view that the animal kingdom was given by God for our use. But she cites a Hindu colleague who took the opposite view, putting the burden of proof on scientists to show that animals are not mentally complex. 'Why should you start out with the idea that animals don't have a theory of mind?' Clayton asks. 'Why not start with the idea that they do?'[5]

Returning to a central theme of this book: how can we regard nests as 'art' when art is something we traditionally associate with museums and galleries, with quiet, ascetic environments and, most importantly, with humankind? Of course, art is far from fixed and constantly challenges its own boundaries. Particularly since the beginning of the twentieth century, attitudes towards what constitutes art have changed radically. In the 1960s, the Land Art movement saw sculpture entering a fresh relationship with nature and a new aesthetic was born.

Robert Smithson's massive *Spiral Jetty* (1970), which he built at remote Rozel Point on the Great Salt Lake, Utah, is the movement's defining work and Smithson's masterpiece. A rough stone and earth causeway, spiralling from the shore, it is four and a half metres wide and 450 metres long. Smithson utilised the materials of the site itself—black basalt rock that he took from the shore and arranged at a height just above sea level so people could walk on the earthwork like a pier. *Spiral Jetty* interacts with its environment. The translucent red water changes colour, from deeper to lighter pink, depending on the amount of algae, and the rocks are subject to shifting levels of salt encrustation which can turn them glistening white. Smithson approved: 'If the work has sufficient physicality, any kind of natural change will tend to enhance [it].'[6] Natural change did occur: the waters of the lake rose (there was a drought when Smithson built it) and covered *Spiral Jetty* for nearly thirty years, but in the past decade it's been visible once more.

From the air, probably the best perspective to view the work, it's an impossibly beautiful, subtle and regal work, one that engages in a calmly considered and elegant dialogue with its natural environment. *Spiral Jetty* does not so much become part of nature as comment *on* nature: what nature offers art and what art can offer nature. The artwork attracts visitors from all over the world. I remember first seeing photographs of it in *Artforum* when I was an undergraduate art history student; I was swept away by the scale, a grand, raw vision that refused to be enclosed by the clean white walls of a gallery.

Many artists have followed Smithson's lead. Andy Goldsworthy is the most prominent and also one of the best-known and most popular artists working today. Goldsworthy uses materials available in the location, works with his hands and, when possible, uses only natural materials. Art writer Ben Tufnell explains that Goldsworthy's modus operandi is not 'ecological purism' but a way to gain an intimate knowledge of place.[7] Goldsworthy regards himself as a formalist, exploring the properties of different materials and engaging with a range of sculptural concepts like mass, balance, space and form. But his forms are richly symbolic: holes and voids, cairns shaped like eggs or seeds, spirals or wandering lines.

The work *Stick Hole, Scaur Water, Dumfriesshire, Scotland, 14 October 1991* (1991) is simple, dramatic and eerie. Scaur Water is a river in Dumfriesshire where Goldsworthy has often worked. There he has constructed a faux nest inside a moss-covered rock grotto. Behind it, the river swirls. Goldsworthy photographs his own work in situ; as commendable a photographer as he is a sculptor, he makes it possible to almost smell the moss and the damp, to hear the cascading water. If you came across this sculpture unawares you might gaze at the nest and wonder what creature had built it. The dark hole at its centre beckons the eye to peer into its secretiveness. The grotto frames the nest, like a huge, gnarled green claw, protecting it, framing it. The nest is so expertly built that I'm not sure if a bird could have done better.

It's ironic that if a nest by a stork, a swallow or any other bird that I've discussed in this book were exhibited as the latest work by Andy Goldsworthy, the art audience would coo over its poetic craftsmanship, its structural form, its clever response to the natural environment, its timely statement about our damaged planet. It might win a major art prize.

The rise of Australian Aboriginal art has also challenged preconceived ideas about artistic practice. The Western Desert art movement, which created the audience and the market for contemporary Aboriginal art, began in the early 1970s at Papunya, around 250 kilometres west of Alice Springs, Australia's red heart. Papunya was the last of the Aboriginal reserves established by the federal government where tribal peoples, predominantly of the Luritja/Pintupi language groups, were forced to live after removal from their traditional lands. An idealistic young art teacher, Geoffrey Bardon, encouraged senior men in the community to paint their Dreamings with acrylic on canvas. In effect, Aboriginal people began making permanent artefacts from traditional designs with Western materials. The originality and beauty of those works not only made the heritage of the Papunya artists accessible to a non-Indigenous audience but also signalled the revitalisation of Aboriginal visual culture.

Aboriginal people, however, do not regard their work as 'art' and do not have a word for art in their languages. That's the definition art lovers and the art market have bequeathed it. Aboriginal pictograms, which were originally drawn in the sand or on the body as part of a ritual, are representations of the land, its shape-shifting Dreamtime beings and the people's time-honoured relationship with both. Emily Kame Kngwarreye, whose lusciously painted and impeccably composed works hang in international museums, has been compared to Monet and Pollock. Emily, as she was known, only began to paint in her eighties. She knew nothing of Western art, had never attended art school and was illiterate in the English language. Yet she 'trained' in the minute observation of the natural world and her lore.

Many of Kngwarreye's paintings take an aerial perspective. This is one of Aboriginal art's most puzzling and fascinating features. Flying into Alice Springs for the first time a few years ago, it seemed as if I was flying over a vast abstract painting. On the red earth with its low hills and salt lakes, its bluffs and boulders, it was as though I could see the tracks, marks and traces of the Dreamtime creatures who made the land and who remain there so powerfully. But I was thousands of metres up where such visions are possible; Aboriginal people paint aerial perspectives automatically and familiarly, though they may never have flown in a plane or seen their country from such a height. The Skyworld features in many Dreamings with descriptions of celestial realms as if they were fully experienced, physical places. Aboriginal art's treatment of space makes it 'readable' and accessible in the language of modern abstract painting, which flattens perspective, modelling and shading to explore the two-dimensionality of the picture plane, and that eschews the object for the symbol. It has attracted an audience that is sophisticated in the techniques and the vocabulary of modern art while Aboriginal art is self-referential, engaged solely in its spiritual tradition, its cosmology.

Modern art has also claimed Indigenous artefacts as art. In 1907, when Picasso saw African tribal masks in Paris, he commented, 'The masks weren't just like any other pieces of sculpture. Not at all. They were magic things.'[8] The masks triggered a catharsis when Picasso quoted them in *Les Demoiselles d'Avignon* (1907, Museum of Modern Art, New York), the painting that was the precedent to Cubism, the movement that shattered the three-dimensional pictorial illusionism that had shaped Western painting since Giotto. Following Picasso's lead, modern art has embraced what was previously deemed 'primitive', discovering potent aesthetic qualities in objects once designated as anthropology. Given such shifts in attitudes towards art and art-making, where does this leave my claim that birds can, in some cases, be considered 'artists'? In terms of technique and virtuosity, birds are second to none. They've had millions of years to perfect their talents, much longer than homo sapiens. Michelangelo painted the Sistine ceiling but he didn't do it with a brush in his mouth and no other form of assistance. Birds' inventiveness is driven by evolution, by the struggle for survival. Art is sometimes regarded as a leisure activity: if a people have the time (and sufficient food and shelter), they can develop the ability to create pleasing and well-made objects. But what if the urge to make things carries with it an inherent desire, in the case of humans and perhaps of some highly intelligent birds, to make those things beautiful? Beauty also needs planning and a discerning audience that can appreciate it. For the lesser masked weavers of Africa, evolution has provided a critical mass. Though the weavers nest in colonies, they don't build apartment houses like their relatives the sociable weavers but self-contained units. The males create elaborate nests resembling pendulous, open-weave baskets that hang one by one from slender branches. As the males work, the females judiciously assess their progress. A great deal of skill and industry goes into each nest: the weave must be of the right tightness and elasticity or the eggs will slide out. When the nest is finished and ready for judging, the male perches hopefully beside it. A messy, disorganised nest, and its designer, will be rejected. The better examples are given a stern and thorough examination, including an interior inspection. If the female approves of the nest's good design and structural qualities she immediately moves in, keeping the continuing standards of nest building among the lesser masked weavers very high. In these competitive stakes, the authority of the female's demanding taste is paramount. Though the females are simply doing the best for their species, you can't help but feel sympathetic towards the males, whose splendid and time-consuming efforts are often met with rejection—especially as rejection in the animal kingdom often means death. If feminists wished to seek a paradigm in nature for female power then species such as the weavers could provide them with one.

Is art a matter of quantifiable intelligence? James Gould is one of the world's leading experts in animal behaviour; he and Carol Grant Gould are the authors of *Animal Architects: Building and the evolution of intelligence*. The Goulds note that bird architecture exhibits an individual variability that 'in humans we would call aesthetic',[9] making the Goulds wonder whether birds' cognitive preferences and tastes could be akin to our own. Together with Darwin, and Attenborough, the Goulds agree that the bowerbird is an artist: 'Bowers are the ultimate example of architectural show, unconstrained by the need for conventional utility.'[10] But, rather like Mike Hansell, they're a little nervous about their conclusions. After all, a 'hard-nosed sceptic' might object, because the bower design and decoration merely indicate 'innate circuitry' in the bird's brain. To the sceptic, any sense of beauty or aesthetic delight is an illusion, 'an artifact of the neural wiring that controls the release of pleasure-inducing chemicals in the brain'[11] of either humans or animals.

Some contemporary philosophers are prepared to make far bolder claims, however. Rather than ask, 'What is art?', they ask instead, 'What is nature?' The influential French duo Gilles Deleuze and Félix Guattari construct a philosophical paradigm that links nature directly with art. 'Perhaps art begins with the animal,' Deleuze and Guattari consider, 'at least with the animal that carves out a territory and constructs a house', or what is called a habitat.[12] They comment on the tooth-billed bowerbird which, each morning, severs leaves from trees, dropping them to the ground, then turns them over so that the paler underside contrasts with the earth: 'in this way [the bird] constructs a stage for itself'. The male then sings a complex song in which, at intervals, it also imitates the notes of other birds. To Deleuze and Guattari the bowerbird is 'a complete artist', because the combination of colours, postures and sounds sketch out 'a total work of art' that we as humans can appreciate.[13] Deleuze and Guattari regard composition as the sole definition of art: if composition is the rule by which we understand what is art, then what is *not* composed, what is haphazard or accidental, 'untouched', can't be a work of art.[14] Art takes nature's profusion and transforms it into something ordered and beautiful. By *framing* nature, by taking a bit of its chaos and subjecting it to the creative process, chaos is transformed into a composition, a design, a work of art that we can appreciate.

Australian philosopher Elizabeth Grosz expands on their views. Taking her cue from Darwin's theory of sexual selection, she believes 'there is much "art" in the natural world'. This includes 'the haunting beauty of birdsong, the provocative performance of erotic displays in primates, the attraction of insects to the perfume of plants' which all go beyond what is needed for mere survival. Grosz considers such acts attest to 'the artistic impact of sexual attraction', which enables the production of 'the frivolous, the unnecessary, the pleasing, the sensory for their own sake'.[15] Sexual selection ensures that art is constantly charged with new possibilities—for example, in the case of weavers and bowerbirds who must build elegant and structurally sound nests to attract a mate.

Grosz isn't concerned with traditional aesthetics. To her, art in all its manifestations is the way that life experiments with nature in order to bring about change. 'Art is not the accomplishment of "higher" existence . . . but an elaboration of the most primitive and elementary fragments of an ancient animal prehistory.'[16]

As an art historian who has written about visual culture from Egypt to Greece to Rome and all the way through to French Impressionism and Aboriginal art, I've experienced both pleasure and discomfort writing this book. The pleasure came easily: I consider the nests objects of beauty and my research has amplified that view. The discomfort came from my inner voices, the ones that awaken me and growl in the night. What would Richard Dawkins say! What will the reviewers say!

She's lost her marbles. If you present aspects of nature in a slightly unorthodox way, there's the prospect that you'll be regarded as a kook or, even worse, a believer. This is perhaps one reason why scientists like Nicky Clayton, James Gould and Mike Hansell hedge their bets. Darwin, to his credit, didn't give a damn.

Richard Dawkins' robust attacks on creationism, advanced in his bestselling books *The God Delusion* and *The Greatest Show on Earth: The evidence for evolution*, meet with my whole-hearted approval. Dawkins has appointed himself as Darwin's defender and I would never disagree with Professor Dawkins, certainly not in his earshot. But Dawkins' target has shifted from the creationists to include anyone who is foolish enough to entertain a belief in the metaphysical. Unless you are an atheist, it seems, you deserve to be ridiculed. Where does that leave Indigenous people whose cultural survival, like that of Australian Aborigines, is directly connected to their spiritual traditions? For Indigenous people, 'culture' means a relationship with country and kinship, and its continuous expression through religious ritual. To them, birds such as the willie wagtail are magical creatures who play an active and important role in their lives.

Despite the apparent bravado of the intellectual class, we're easily unnerved. The last thing we ever want to look is passé. Recently I overheard a distinguished professor, who is also a very nice fellow, murmur to another academic, 'Do you realise some of our colleagues are *non-atheists*?' I mention this, not in support of atheism or non-atheism, but to point out how easy it is to be regarded as a curiosity, an outsider, to be consigned, metaphorically speaking, to the loony bin, or the dustbin of history.

The major philosophical movement after the Second World War was Existentialism. Its proponents were a cadre of brilliant French intellectuals that included Jean-Paul Sartre, Simone de Beauvoir and Albert Camus. Existentialism claimed that life was absurd, meaningless, but that each individual should take personal responsibility and struggle against the tide of alienation, boredom and despair, to try to give meaning to his or her own life. In the post-Holocaust West of the 1950s, the era of the Cold War with its threat of nuclear annihilation, Existentialism's claims resounded, especially with a younger generation. Not nihilistic but pessimistic, Existentialism banished transcendence as effete nonsense.

Surrealism had been the major cultural avant-garde movement before the Second World War. Under the jurisdiction of

André Breton, it embraced painting, film, photography and poetry, and its luminaries included Salvador Dalí, Max Ernst, Luis Buñuel and René Magritte. Picasso and Marcel Duchamp were fellow travellers. Breton, like many of the Surrealists, had fled Paris for New York when the Nazis invaded France. On his return to Europe, he tried to re-establish Surrealism. An idealistic movement, it charted the dream, the unconscious and the occult, exploring the very outposts of imaginative thinking. Surrealism was in love with love, the more romantic and erotic the better. At that time, Breton had committed himself to the study of shamanism, Native American artefacts and initiation myths. He believed that humanity needed a spiritual component to rebuild postwar society. But Breton found himself up against Sartre, the new kid on the block, who placed reality squarely in the realm of the conscious. From the vantage point of *Les temps modernes*, the radical newspaper he'd founded, Sartre, a Stalinist, dismissed Surrealism as a phenomenon from the era of the First World War 'like the Charleston or the yo-yo'.[17] To the Existentialists, Surrealism was frivolous, apolitical and promoted mysticism and religiosity.

In the early 1970s, when I was in my early twenties, I began to publish art criticism. I was a fanatical formalist and devoted to the views of Clement Greenberg, the influential American critic. His view was that art was purely for art's sake. Subject matter, let alone the artist's gender, was irrelevant. Realism was taboo and abstraction the benchmark of the progressive artist. A painting referred to its own inherent, material qualities—it was a flat, two-dimensional object and to pretend it was a window into a third dimension, or a vehicle for social comment, was baloney.

Using the occasional personal pronoun was, I considered, daringly intimate. I regarded Surrealism as vague, intangible and wishy-washy. As for Dalí's paintings, how vulgar, how kitsch! At that time, I remember meeting another critic who told me that, after reading my criticism, he expected that I would be at least fifty, wearing a bun and horn-rimmed glasses. Perversely, I was flattered: it meant I was 'tough'. But eventually I became disenchanted with the predictable nature of the art about which I wrote. I felt stultified and trapped by a spurious historical determinism, sailing down the mainstream of no return. Feminism and the rise of the women's art movement enabled me to discover that I could respond to and admire a range of art that I'd previously dismissed as lowbrow, trivial or decorative. My writing style subsequently relaxed and became more personal, humorous and unencumbered by jargon—rather like much of the art I enjoyed. Indeed, despite Existentialism's attacks on Surrealism, it was rehabilitated as a significant force in the cultural history of the twentieth century. Today it's more popular and relevant than Existentialism and, I might add, Greenbergian formalism.

Early in 2011, I visited the Gallery of Modern Art in Brisbane. I went there for the birds. Finches, to be precise. As part of a large survey titled '21st Century: Art in the first decade', French artist Céleste Boursier-Mougenot had created a mesmerising installation called *From Here to Ear (v.13)*. In the large, light gallery, live gouldian finches created an ambient soundscape as they alighted on 'branches' of coat hangers that hung from five octagonal harpsichords installed in the ceiling. The combined sound was a counterpoint: the low, resonant hum from the wires together with the birds' constant, cheerful chirruping. As one journalist commented, 'For its sheer beauty, subtle ingenuity and complexity of ideas the installation is probably the exhibition's star work.'[18] Four species of finches were involved—zebra, double-bar, gouldian and crimson—all under the watchful eye of the Queensland Finch Society. Lightweight, roofed cane nests had been constructed for them, and seeds, grasses and clean water were supplied. When I visited the exhibition, the finches were having a ball. Relieved of predators, inclement weather and the need to find sustenance and shelter, they could eat, flit, chat and play to their hearts' content. Like me, other visitors were enchanted—especially the children, whose faces opened in wonder and delight when they entered the gallery. A group of schoolgirls stood stock-still with their arms outstretched, laughing, hoping the birds would alight on them.

I noticed that some of the birds had adorned their nests with grasses. Others didn't bother. One couple disdained the purpose-built nest and were busily arranging grasses on the highest surface they could find: a flat aluminium light shield. (The globe was off so it wasn't hot.) It was a laborious and entirely unsuccessful operation. The grass simply slid off and fell to the floor. But the finches did not desist. I visited the installation on several occasions and each time they were at it, while the gallery staff patiently cleaned up the grass that accumulated on the floor below. Apart from the unique beauty of *From Here to Ear*, it also gave me the opportunity to observe species of birds that I'd never be able to see up close in the wild. Perhaps Boursier-Mougenot suggests a future where artistic projects, based on birds' aesthetics combined with our own, can produce moving and exquisite works of art. We have much to learn from them.

It's evening as I finish and I can hear the blackbird carolling with all the beauty and arrogance of an opera singer. Dear reader, I hope you have enjoyed the voyage. Enough of words. I'm going out to listen.

Notes

Chapter 1

1 Italo Calvino, *Mr Palomar*, Martin Secker and Warburg, London, 1985, p. 47.

2 Charles Darwin, *The Descent of Man and Selection in Relation to Sex*, [1879], introduction by James Moore and Adrian Desmond, Penguin Books, London, 2004, p. 115.

3 Virginia Morell, 'Build it and they will come: Bowerbirds,' *National Geographic*, July 2010, p. 73.

4 Lyanda Lynn Haupt, *Pilgrim on the Great Bird Continent: The importance of everything and other lessons from Darwin's lost notebooks*, Little, Brown and Company, New York and Boston, 2006, p. 119.

5 Charles Darwin (ed.), *The Zoology of the Voyage of HMS Beagle During the years 1832–1836 under the command of*

    Captain Fitzroy, R.N., Vol. III, Birds by John Gould,
    Facsimile Reprint, Nova Pacifica, Wellington, 1980, p. 17.

6 Quoted in Haupt, *Pilgrim on the Great Bird Continent:* p. 115.

7 Haupt, *Pilgrim on the Great Bird Continent*, p. 126.

8 Mike Hansell, *Built by Animals: The natural history of animal architecture*, Oxford University Press, Oxford, 2007, p. 227.

9 Darwin, *The Descent of Man*, p. 114.

10 Hansell, *Built by Animals*, p. 233.

Chapter 2

1 Adrian Desmond and James Moore, *Darwin: The life of a tormented evolutionist*, W.W. Norton & Company, New York and London, 1991, p. 209.

2 Janet Browne, *Charles Darwin, Voyaging*, Princeton University Press, Princeton, New Jersey, 1995, p. 361

3 Charles Darwin (ed.), *The Zoology of the Voyage of HMS Beagle During the years 1832–1836 under the command of Captain Fitzroy, R.N.*, Vol. III, Birds by John Gould, Facsimile Reprint, Nova Pacifica, Wellington, 1980, p. B.

4 Alec H. Chisholm, *The Story of Elizabeth Gould*, Hawthorn Press, Melbourne, 1944, p. 49.

5 Gould, *The Birds of Australia*, Vol. II, n.p.

6 Gould, *The Birds of Australia*, Vol. II, n.p.

7 Chisholm, *The Story of Elizabeth Gould*, p. 33.

8 Gould, *The Birds of Australia*, Vol. III, n.p.

9 Gould, *The Birds of Australia*, Vol. VII, n.p.

10 Kenn Kaufman, 'Small miracles', *Audobon Magazine*, March–April 2008. http://audobonmagazine.org/

features0803/truenature.html. (Accessed 20 September 2010.) See also www.sharonbeals.com.

11 Kaufman, 'Small miracles'.

Chapter 3

1 Pat Shipman, *Taking Wing: Archaeopteryx and the evolution of bird flight*, Simon & Schuster, New York, 1998, pp. 15–16.

2 Shipman, *Taking Wing*, p. 14.

3 John R. Horner and James Gorman, *Digging Dinosaurs*, Harper & Row, New York, 1988, p. 63.

4 http://museumvictoria.com.au/collections-research/ our-research/sciences/staff/thomas-h-rich. (Accessed 2 November 2010.)

5 Charles Dickens, *Barnaby Rudge, A Tale of the Riots of 'Eighty*, Oxford University Press, London, 1954, pp. xxiii.

6 *The Epic of Gilgamesh*, trans. and introduction by N.K. Sandars, Penguin, Harmondsworth, 1964, p. 108.

7 Ovid, *Metamorphoses*, trans. and introduction by Mary M. Innes, Penguin, Harmondsworth, 1955, p. 64.

8 Marie Woolf, 'Executions are back at Tower with secret cull to prevent a legendary fall', 28 February 2005. www. independent.co.uk/.../executions-are-back-at-tower-with- secret-cull-to-<wbr>prevent-a-legendary-fall. (Accessed 12 November 2010.)

9 Bernd Heinrich, *Mind of the Raven: Investigations and adventures with wolf-birds*, HarperCollins, New York, 2000, p. 254.

10 Charles Wohlforth, 'Who are you calling bird brain?', *Discover*, March 2010, p. 47.

11 Wohlforth, 'Who are you calling bird brain?', p. 46.

12 Wohlforth, 'Who are you calling bird brain?', pp. 48–9.

13 Email to the author from Nicky Clayton, 24 December 2010.

14 www.youtube.com/watch?v=y_MnwNyXODs. (Accessed 15 November 2010.)

15 Rambert Dance Company won the 2010 Laurence Olivier award for outstanding performance. Nicky Clayton is now scientific adviser to the company.

16 'A Comedy of Change Rambert Dance Company Ballet in collaboration with Professor Nicky Clayton', *Cambridge Neuroscience*, 29 August 2009.

17 Lyanda Lynn Haupt, *Crow Planet: Essential wisdom from the urban wilderness*, Little, Brown and Company, New York and Boston, 2009, pp. 114–15.

Chapter 4

1 *The Diary of Virginia Woolf*, Anne Olivier Bell (ed.) and Andrew McNeillie (assistant ed.), Penguin Books, London, 1982, vol. III, 1925–1930: 12 August 1928, p. 191.

2 Leonard Woolf quoted in Victoria Glendinning, *Leonard Woolf*, Simon & Schuster, London, 2006, p. 135.

3 Virginia Woolf, *Between the Acts*, annotated and with an introduction by Melba Cuddy-Keane, Harcourt, New York, 2008, p. 26.

4 Woolf, *Between the Acts*, pp. 20, 31.

5   Woolf, *Between the Acts*, pp. 3, 6.

6   Woolf, *Between the Acts*, p. 45.

7   Woolf, *Between the Acts*, p. 7.

8   Woolf, *Between the Acts*, p. 70.

9   Woolf, *Between the Acts*, pp. 71, 75.

10 Guilhem Lesaffre, *Taking Flight: Journeys of migration*, Hachette, London, 2003, p. 22.

11 Royal Society for the Protection of Birds: Swallow: Migration. www.rspb.org.uk/wildlife/birdguide/name/s/ swallow/migration.aspx. (Accessed 23 November 2010.)

12 Jonathan Elphick (ed.), *The Atlas of Bird Migration: Tracing the great journeys of the world's birds*, Marshall Editions, London, 1995, p. 32.

13 Adebayo Adedeji, 'The swallow roosts of southeast Nigeria', www.safariweb.com/safarimate/trial2/swallow.htm. (Accessed 26 November 2010.)

14 James L. Gould and Carol Grant Gould, *Animal Architects: Building and the evolution of intelligence*, Basic Books, New York, 2007, p. 182.

15 *The Diary of Virginia Woolf*, Anne Olivier Bell (ed.) and Andrew McNeillie (assistant ed.), Penguin Books, London, 1985, vol. V, 1936–1940: 24 December 1940, p. 346.

16 Virginia Woolf to John Lehmann, [27? March 1941], *Leave the Letters Till We're Dead, The Letters of Virginia Woolf*, Nigel Nicolson (ed.) and Joanne Trautmann (assistant ed.), Hogarth Press, London, 1994, vol. VI, 1936–1941: p. 486.

17 Virginia Woolf to Vanesssa Bell, [23? March 1941], *Leave the Letters Till We're Dead*, p. 485.

18 Karen Blixen, *Out of Africa*, Jonathan Cape, London, [1937] 1975, pp. 3, 7.

19 Isak Dinesen, *Letters from Africa, 1914–1931*, Frans Lasson (ed.) for the Rungstedlund Foundation, trans. Anne Born, University of Chicago Press, Chicago, 1981: 19 May 1917, p. 44.

20 Blixen, *Out of Africa*, p. 292.

21 Dinesen, *Letters from Africa*: 15 March 1924, p. 196; 19 August 1923, p. 169.

22 Blixen, *Out of Africa*, p. 347; Dinesen, *Letters from Africa*: 10 April 1931, pp. 418–19.

23 Dinesen, *Letters from Africa*: 2 September 1928, p. 379; 14 September 1930, p. 410.

24 Dinesen, *Letters from Africa*: 2 September 1928, p. 378.

25 Hans Christian Andersen, *The Complete Fairy Tales*, Wordsworth Editions, Ware, Hertfordshire, 1997, p. 183.

26 Andersen, *The Complete Fairy Tales*, pp. 184–5.

27 Andersen, *The Complete Fairy Tales*, p. 185

28 Blixen, *Out of Africa*, pp. 270–71.

29 Blixen, *Out of Africa*, p. 271.

30 Isak Dinesen, *Daguerreotypes and Other Essays*, Heinemann, London, 1979, pp. 202, 209.

31 Lietuvos Ortinologų Dragua, www.ciconia. lt/?=EN&content=news&id=97. (Accessed 10 December 2010.)

32 Lietuvos Ortinologų Dragua, www.ciconia. lt/?=EN&content=news&id=97. (Accessed 10 December 2010.)

33 Lietuvos Ortinologų Dragua, www.ciconia.
    lt/?=EN&content=news&id=97. (Accessed 10 December
    2010.)

34 Andy Rouse, *Concepts of Nature: A wildlife photographer's
    art*, Argentum, London, 2008, p. 123.

35 Dinesen, *Daguerreotypes*, p. 12.

Chapter 5

1   Kenneth Neill Cameron, *Shelley: The golden years*, Harvard
    University Press, Cambridge, 1974, p. 425.

2   Caesar R. Blake (ed.), *The Recognition of Emily Dickinson:
    Selected criticism since 1890*, University of Michigan Press,
    Ann Arbor, 1964, p. 45.

3   *The Letters of Emily Dickinson*, Thomas H. Johnson (ed.)
    and Theodora Ward (associate ed.), Belknap Press, Harvard
    University, Cambridge, 1958, vol. II, p. 546.

4   *The Letters of Emily Dickinson*, vol. III, p. 672.

5   Judith Farr, *The Passion of Emily Dickinson*, Harvard
    University Press, Cambridge and London, 1992, p. ix.

6   *The Letters of Emily Dickinson*, vol. I, p. 216.

7   Quoted in Farr, *The Passion of Emily Dickinson*, p. 10.

8   Quoted in Jonathan Bate, *John Clare: A biography*, Farrar,
    Straus and Giroux, New York, 2003, p. 109.

9   Quoted in Bate, *John Clare*, p. 189.

10 Quoted in Stephen Gill, *William Wordsworth: A life*, Oxford
    University Press, Oxford, 1989, p. 15.

11 Gill, *William Wordsworth*, p. 36.

12 William Wordsworth, *The Prelude, 1799, 1805, 1850*,
    Jonathan Wordsworth, M.H. Abrams and Stephen Gill
    (eds), W.W. Norton and Company, New York, 1979: 1805,
    Prelude, Book VI, lines 201–3, p. 196.
13 Quoted in Gill, *William Wordsworth*, p. 36.
14 Quoted in Gill, *William Wordsworth*, p. 43.

Chapter 6

1 Ovid, *Metamorphoses*, trans. and introduction by Mary
   M. Innes, Penguin, Penguin, Harmondsworth, (1955) 1983,
   p. 136.
2 Ovid, *Metamorphoses*, p. 138.
3 Ovid, *Metamorphoses*, p. 18.
4 Charles Wolhlforth, 'Who are you calling bird brain?',
   Discover, March 2010, p. 48.
5 Wolhlforth, 'Who are you calling bird brain?', p. 48.
6 David Bourdon, *Designing the Earth: The human impulse to
   shape nature*, Harry N. Abrams, New York, 1995, p. 118.
7 Ben Tufnell, *Land Art*, Tate Publishing, London, 2006, p. 82.
8 Picasso quoted in John Richardson, with the collaboration
   of Marilyn McCully, *A Life of Picasso, Vol II, 1907–1917*,
   Jonathon Cape, London, 1996, p. 24.
9 Gould and Gould, *Animal Architects: Building and the
   evolution of intelligence*, Basic Books, New York, 2007,
   p. 218.
10 Gould and Gould, *Animal Architects*, p. 248.
11 James L. Gould and Carol Grant Gould, *Animal Architects*,
    p. 247.

12 Gilles Deleuze and Félix Guattari, *What is Philosophy?*, trans. Hugh Tomlinson and Graham Burchell, Columbia University Press, New York, 1994, p. 183.

13 Deleuze and Guattari, *What is Philosophy?*, p. 184.

14 Deleuze and Guattari, *What is Philosophy?*, p. 191.

15 Elizabeth Grosz, *Chaos, Territory, Art: Deleuze and the framing of the earth*, Columbia University Press, New York, 2008, p. 7.

16 Grosz, *Chaos, Territory, Art*, p. 35.

17 Mark Polizzotti, *Revolution of the Mind: The life of André Breton*, Black Widow Press, Boston, 2009, p. 485.

18 Gabriella Coslovich, '21st Century: Art in the first decade', *The Age*, 4 January 2011. www.theage.com.au. (Accessed 23 October 2011.)

Bibliography

Hans Christian Andersen, *The Complete Fairy Tales*, Wordsworth Editions, Ware, Hertfordshire, 1997.

David Attenborough, *The Life of Birds*, BBCTV, DVD, 1998.

Jonathan Bate, *John Clare: A biography*, Farrar, Straus and Giroux, New York, 2003.

The Diary of Virginia Woolf, Anne Olivier Bell (ed.) and Andrew McNeillie (assistant ed.), Penguin Books, London, 1982, vol. III: 1925–1930.

The Diary of Virginia Woolf, Anne Olivier Bell (ed.) and Andrew McNeillie (assistant ed.), Penguin Books, London, 1985, vol. V: 1936–1941.

Karen Blixen, *Out of Africa*, Jonathan Cape, London, [1937], 1975.

David Bourdon, *Designing the Earth: The human impulse to shape nature*, Harry N. Abrams, New York, 1995.

Janet Browne, *Charles Darwin: Voyaging*, Princeton University Press, Princeton, New Jersey, 1995.

Janine Burke, *Source: Nature's healing role in art and writing*, Allen & Unwin, Sydney, 2009.

Kenneth Carpenter, *Eggs, Nests and Baby Dinosaurs: A look at dinosaur reproduction*, Indiana University Press, Bloomington, 1999.

Alec H. Chisholm, *The Story of Elizabeth Gould*, Hawthorn Press, Melbourne, 1944.

Mark Cocker, *Crow Country: A meditation on birds, landscape and nature*, Jonathan Cape, London, 2007.

Charles Darwin, *On the Origin of Species By Means of Natural Selection, or the Preservation of Favoured Races in the Struggle for Life*, (1859), introduction by Sir Julian Huxley, Signet Classics, New York, 2003.

——*The Descent of Man and Selection in Relation to Sex*, (1879), introduction by James Moore and Adrian Desmond, Penguin Books, London, 2004.

——(ed.), *The Zoology of the Voyage of HMS Beagle During the years 1832–1836 under the command of Captain Fitzroy, R.N.*, Vol. III, Birds by John Gould, Facsimile Reprint, Nova Pacifica, Wellington, 1980.

Gilles Deleuze and Félix Guattari, *What is Philosophy?*, trans. Hugh Tomlinson and Graham Burchell, Columbia University Press, New York, 1994.

Adrian Desmond and James Moore, *Darwin: The life of a tormented evolutionist*, W.W. Norton & Company, New York: London, 1991.

Jonathan Elphick (ed.), *The Atlas of Bird Migration: Tracing the great journeys of the world's birds*, Marshall Editions, London, 1995.

Judith Farr, *The Passion of Emily Dickinson*, Harvard University Press, Cambridge: London, 1992.

Stephen Gill, *William Wordsworth: A life*, Oxford University Press, Oxford, 1989.

James L. Gould and Carol Grant Gould, *Animal Architects: Building and the evolution of intelligence*, Basic Books, New York, 2007.

John Gould, *The Birds of Australia*, John Gould, London, 1848, vols I–VII.

Elizabeth Grosz, *Chaos, Territory, Art: Deleuze and the framing of the earth*, Columbia University Press, New York, 2008.

Mike Hansell, *Built by Animals: The natural history of animal architecture*, Oxford University Press, Oxford, 2007.

Open Me Carefully: Emily Dickinson's letters to Susan Huntington Dickinson, Ellen Louise Hart and Martha Nell Smith (eds), Paris Press, Ashfield, 1998.

Lyanda Lynn Haupt, *Crow Planet: Essential wisdom from the urban wilderness*, Little, Brown and Company, New York: Boston, 2009.

——*Pilgrim on the Great Bird Continent: The importance of everything and other lessons from Darwin's lost notebooks*, Little, Brown and Company, New York: Boston, 2006.

Bernd Heinrich, *Mind of the Raven: Investigations and adventures with wolf-birds*, HarperCollins, New York, 2000.

John R. Horner and James Gorman, *Digging Dinosaurs*, Harper & Row, New York, 1988.

"I Am": The selected poetry of John Clare, Jonathan Bate (ed.), Farrar, Straus and Giroux, New York, 2003.

Ovid, *Metamorphoses*, trans. and intro. Mary M. Innes, Penguin, Harmondsworth, (1955), 1983

The Letters of Emily Dickinson, Thomas H. Johnson (ed.) and Theodora Ward (assoc. ed.), Belknap Press, Harvard University, Cambridge, 1958, 3 vols.

Kenn Kaufman, 'Small Miracles', *Audobon Magazine*, March–April, 2008.

Guilhem Lesaffre, *Taking Flight: Journeys of migration*, Hachette, London, 2003.

Life, Narrated by David Attenborough, BBCTV, DVD, 2010.

Leave the Letters Till We're Dead: The letters of Virginia Woolf, Nigel Nicolson (ed.) and Joanne Trautmann (assistant ed.), Hogarth Press, London, 1994, vol. VI: 1936–1941.

Andy Rouse, *Concepts of Nature: A wildlife photographer's art*, Argentum, London, 2008.

The Epic of Gilgamesh, trans. and intro. N.K. Sandars, Penguin, Harmondsworth, 1960.

Aaran Sharf, *Art and Photography*, Penguin, Harmondsworth, 1974.

Pat Shipman, *Taking Wing: Archaeopteryx and the evolution of bird flight*, Simon and Schuster, New York, 1998.

Isabella Tree, *The Bird Man: The extraordinary story of John Gould*, Ebury Press, London, 1991.

Ben Tufnell, *Land Art*, Tate Publishing, London, 2006.

Charles Wolhlforth, 'Who are you calling bird brain?', *Discover*, March, 2010.

Virginia Woolf, *Between the Acts*, (1941), annotated and with an introduction by Melba Cuddy-Keane, Harcourt, New York, 2008.

Acknowledgements

I WOULD LIKE TO THANK Jane Palfreyman, my publisher, and Patricia Vickers-Rich, Monash University, for their enthusiastic responses to the idea for this book. Thanks are also due to Nicky Clayton, Cambridge University, for her encouragement and also for reading sections of the manuscript. Sharon Beals, that great photographer of nests, generously responded to my queries.

To Penny Olsen, AM, Australian National University, I owe a special debt of gratitude. Professor Olsen is one of Australia's most distinguished ornithologists. Her careful reading of the manuscript and her invaluable comments corrected many errors. I would also like to thank James Gould, Princeton University, for his kind comments after reading a chapter.

David Sheehy, Monash University, has produced some excellent photography. I'd also like to thank Richard Overell, Rare Books, Matheson Library, Monash University and Wayne Longmore, Collections Manager, Ornithology and Mammalogy, Melbourne Museum, for their assistance. Staff at the Discovery Centre, Melbourne Museum were also helpful. Lynda Chapple ably assisted in tracking down permissions. Clara Finlay, my copy-editor, made any number of sensitive and useful suggestions.

Most particularly, I am indebted to Monash University for awarding me a research fellowship that made it possible to write this book.

Permissions

I ACKNOWLEDGE COPYRIGHT PERMISSIONS FROM the Rungstedlund Foundation (for Karen Blixen); Rachel Woolfson (for Tim Laman's photograph); Andy Rouse and Tim Harris (for Andy Rouse's photograph); Sharon Beals; Gesine Steiner, Museum für Naturkunde Leibniz-Institut für Evolutions-und Biodiversitätsforschung an der Humboldt-Universität, Berlin (for *Archaeopteryx*); Elyse Goldberg, James Gorman Gallery, New York (for Robert Smithson's *Spiral Jetty*); George Steinmetz (for Robert Smithson's *Spiral Jetty*); Viscopy (for Robert Smithson's *Spiral Jetty*). Excerpts from *The Diary of Virginia Woolf*, edited by Anne Olivier Bell, published by Hogarth Press/from *The Letters of Virginia Woolf*, edited by Nigel Nicolson and Joanne Trautmann, published by Hogarth

Index